Caught in the Crossfire

Witnessing a Battle Between Angels and Demons

By Christa Sherman

Christa M. Sherman
3/21/21
John 3:16

Copyright 2020 Christa Sherman. No part of this can be used or copied without permission from the author.

ISBN: 9798579649973

All references to and passages quoted from the Holy Bible are from the New International Version (NIV), English Standard Version (ESV), the New King James Version (NKJV) or the King James (KJ).

Writing consultant: Darla Noble www.dnoblewrites.com

DEDICATION

TO: God. Thank you for loving and forgiving me when I least deserved it. Thank you for sending Jesus to die on the cross for my sins so that forgiveness is even possible. God, I put this book in your hands with the hope that you will allow it to be used to speak to countless readers for their good and for your glory.

TO: Pastor Van Savell for his selfless contribution of knowledge, time, and support.

TO: My family. May you spend your life loving God with all your heart, soul mind, and strength (Mark 12:20).

TO: You, my readers. I pray that you have an open heart and mind as you read my story. If you do not yet know God, I pray that these details of my life cause you to want to know him. And for those of you who have accepted God as your heavenly Father and Jesus as your Savior, I pray that these words inspire you to draw closer to him.

Table of Contents

A Note from the Author	1
Part One	
Chapter 1: Fun with Friends	5
Chapter 2: Opportunity Knocks	11
Chapter 3: Unwanted Visitors	17
Chapter 4: Too Much to Handle	27
Chapter 5: Trudging Along	35
Chapter 6: Bob's Visit	45
Chapter 7: Searching for Answers	49
Chapter 8: God is Very Real	55
Chapter 9: A Test of Faith	63
Chapter 10: God Sends Reinforcements	71
Chapter 11: The Afterlife	81
Part Two	
Chapter 12: Satan and His Adversaries	89
Chapter 13: God's Army of Heavenly Angels	103
Chapter 14: Relentless Pursuit...Relentless Protection	119
Chapter 15: God is Always There	135
Part Three	
Chapter 16: Jesus, the Victor	147
Chapter 17: Are You Lost	161
Chapter 18: Tell Others	167
Final Thoughts	171

A note from the author:

We are at war! Almost since the beginning of time Satan and his demons have been battling God and His angels. The war is constant and ongoing—even now—and will continue until the day of judgment. We live among the rubble and casualties of this war. Sometimes we are among the wounded in this war. And if you have given your life to Jesus and accepted the gift of salvation offered by God through Jesus, you are the spoils Satan and his demons are after. I know this is true, because a) the Bible tells us it is, and b) because I have lived it.

Yes, this story is personal. It is an account of events in which I found myself in the middle of Satan's war against God. I experienced attacks from Satan—attacks that left me scared and feeling helpless and confused. But true to His promise, God rescued me. But just as any other blessing is meant to be shared and 'paid forward', I am convinced that God wants me to share this story with you for the purpose of witnessing to you the truth that Satan is alive and active. That he has his sights set on you. That he is relentless in his pursuit, and that he has an arsenal of weapons to choose from in order to try to take you down.

I am not an expert on the subject of angels and demons. I am only an expert on what I have personally witnessed and experienced. Because of, and through these experiences, God has used His Word and His active presence in my life to teach me to be aware of and on guard against Satan and his demons. In fact, God's Word is the backbone of my story. The facts of the events I have lived can all be supported and explained by scripture. This is important to me because my purpose in telling my story is to remind, teach, and warn you of the reality of Satan and his evil character. So, while this book is extremely personal, I have written it as objectively and accurately as possible. However, I have changed or omitted the names of some people and places in order to protect and respect their privacy and for matters of confidentiality.

Part I

The Awakening

Chapter 1: Fun with Friends

I was somewhere in the middle between being asleep and awake; unaware of the truths that were before me. They weren't anything new. In fact, they have been around since the beginning of time. As things progressed, I wondered how I missed them? I thought I knew enough about God, but in reality, I was as good as blind. My perception of reality wasn't really real. I just didn't know it. Yet.

Since it's always best to start at the beginning, that's what I'll do. I'll start by giving you a little insight as to who I was 'before'. I was an ordinary girl who lived in the small town of Rapid River in the Upper Peninsula of Michigan (also known as the U.P). That makes me a Yooper; a term coined by out of state folks referring to those native to the U.P. For those who aren't well-versed in the geography of this part of the country, the U.P. is nestled between Canada and Wisconsin and is surrounded by the Great Lakes. This geographical oddity makes Michigan unique compared to other states because the top and bottom of our state is completely separated by Lake Michigan. The Mackinac Bridge, an impressive 5-mile bridge across Lake Michigan, is the only thing that connects the U.P with the lower peninsula of Michigan.

FYI: If you ever want to get some Yoopers riled up, then leave us off the map. And yes, this happens occasionally, but when it does, we aren't shy about letting people know about it.

Anyway...

The upper peninsula of Michigan is full of many small towns established a long time ago because of the copper and iron ore mines in the area. Mining isn't the only thing the U.P has to offer. The area is rich with large forests, lakes, rivers, hills, and farmland. Hunting, fishing, hiking, biking, skiing, snowmobiling, and camping are just a handful of things we do in the U.P. for fun. I might as well tell you now that my biggest pet peeve is hearing someone utter the words, "I'm bored." It is my theory that people who claim to be bored lack an imagination. There is always something to do.

You are probably wondering what the charms of the U.P. and my little town have to do with angels and demons. Directly speaking, nothing, really. But looking back later on in my life, I realized that a night spent with friends in a dark campground in search of a ghost, was the first time I entertained the thought that ghosts, spirits, and other such things pertaining to the afterlife were real...or at least a possibility.

It was the summer of 2006. I was 24 years old, a college student on break, and working as a waitress. My friends and I spent every moment of our free time looking for our 'next' adventure. Being bored wasn't in our repertoire. We explored old Indian burial grounds, a local cave, abandoned buildings, and even dug up treasures in an old dump. I've always tried to make the most of every summer because it's my favorite time of year. This one was no exception, but it was also special or significant because I knew that my days as a carefree college student were coming to a close.

What I didn't realize was that this summer would also be significant because it was my last summer of being a carefree, naïve, young woman blind to the actual evil in this world. It happened like this…

One night my much-younger cousin Samantha, and my coworkers, Rietta, Cassie, and Liz decided we were going to go on a ghost hunting adventure.

"Rietta! What are you doing?" I yelled almost angrily. I was not sure I could hold the door handle much longer. My hands were weak and sweaty. The intense pounding on the walls of the outhouse continued with only two inches of plywood separating us from them!

Just moments earlier we were riding along in my tan Chevy Cavalier headed for my favorite campground, Twin Springs. It was dark, but I could have found my way around that place with my eyes closed. I had spent many summers there with my parents and friends, so I didn't have a care or worry in the world. And as my car neared the end of the second loop of campsites, our excitement peaked when we realized site 29 was empty, so it could be ours for the night.

You see, according to legend, the site was haunted. The story was that a guy was sleeping in a tent with his three blonde granddaughters. Sometime during the night, he happened to wake up and saw one of his granddaughters change into what he described as a burnt Indian girl. The end. That was as far as the story went.

Pretty lame, right? My guess is that the story was passed down so many times, that the details began disappearing or changing so much no one knew for sure what to say, so they didn't say anything. But it was enough to convince us we were to have a ghost encounter, so here we were.

Cassie and Liz told us they would be late, so we weren't surprised they weren't there yet. We decided to make a quick run to the outhouse before setting up our gear for the night, so with flashlights in hand, Rietta, Samantha, and I headed down the dark path. We chattered away as our imaginations ran wild in anticipation of what the night would bring. By the time we got there we'd talked ourselves into such a frenzy that we piled into the outhouse together like a bunch of scared little chickens.

We barely had the door closed behind us when something or someone started pounding on the outhouse walls.

"Who is it?" I nervously asked. No answer! Suddenly whoever it was tried to open the locked door. Samantha and I grabbed the handle to keep it closed, but as the pounding continued, our hearts started beating faster and our palms got sweatier. We finally lost our grip and just started screaming.

That's when I turned and saw Rietta sitting on the toilet smoking that cigarette. Almost at the exact time I basically yelled at her, we heard a burst of uncontrollable laughter. It was Cassie and Liz!

After our hearts stopped pounding and we were breathing normally again, we had to admit they'd gotten one over on us, and we all had a pretty good laugh over it. The rest of the night consisted of sitting around the campfire telling stories until almost daybreak—all the while waiting for something to happen. But other than a couple of guys from work who knew our plans and tried unsuccessfully to scare us, the night was uneventful. In other words, no ghost.

Was I surprised? No. But what's even more important is the fact that I would have been equally 'not surprised' had we actually encountered that ghost. At the time I really didn't think too much about what that meant, but like I said, looking back, I now realize that was the night I opened myself up to the possibility (truth) that ghosts or spirits are real. It was also a night I look back on and scold myself for taking such a flippant attitude about seeking out a ghost, because if I'd known then, what I know now…. Well, suffice it to say it wouldn't have happened. There wouldn't have been anything remotely associated with ghosts going on that night or any other night.

Chapter 2: Opportunity Knocks

Life went on (as it is in the habit of doing) and for the most part, if you would have asked me to do so, this small-town Yooper would have described my life as 'good'. Words like 'normal' and 'on track' would have also possibly been included. That's why when my long-time friend, Kimberly, called me in August of 2010, I had no reason to have anything other than *good* thoughts. It had been a while since we had talked, so it was great to hear from her.

You know how that goes. After high school we both got busy with college, jobs, and at this point, both of us were raising two kids. Fortunately, though, Kimberly and I are the kind of friends that can go long periods of time without talking but pick wherever we left off last time as if we'd been together only days before. I'm sure that's because we were pretty much joined at the hip growing up. We lived about a mile apart, which means our bicycle tires got more than the average amount of wear and tear on them riding back and forth between each other's houses *and* all the other countless miles we rode here and there. Hearing her voice was like being transported back in time. Building forts, jumping on and off the bales of hay in her barn, camping out on the trampoline giggling, talking, and counting how many shooting stars we could see....

"Hello?" she asked. "You still there?"

"Yes," I replied. "What's up?"

She asked if I would be interested in assisting an elderly lady part-time in her home in Gladstone, which was just seven miles away. You bet I would! I was delighted that she had thought of me for the job. My goal was to stay at home with my two children rather than putting them in daycare, so this might be the perfect solution. Kimberly said the elderly lady was looking for someone to stay at her house during the night in case she needed anything. I would be able to go to her house when my kids were asleep and sleep myself. The job sounded perfect!

I didn't hesitate for a second to let Kimberly know just how interested I was and to get the lady's contact information. After saying goodbye to Kimberly, I called and scheduled a meeting with the lady, whose name was Hazel, and her son Bob, for two days later.

Have you ever said, or heard someone say, "If I'd known then, what I know now...."? That's the best way I know how to sum up August 3, 2010—the day I got a phone call from Kimberly that I believed was going to let me accomplish one of the most important goals I had set for myself as a parent. I had no idea, though, that that phone call would eventually change my life. More accurately, it would turn my life upside down, inside out, and every other direction.

Hazel lived in a rather impressive house. As I drove down her long, paved driveway, I couldn't help but notice the spacious yard that was freshly mowed and well maintained. There were also large pine, maple and birch trees dotting the landscape, along with multiple kinds of shrubs and flowers. You could just tell by looking at them that they had been lovingly planted and cared for. In a lot of ways, I felt like I was staring at a beautiful painting, which is ironic (not really), because I later learned Hazel was an excellent painter who proudly described her home as 'her canvas.'

When I parked my car and got out, I soon realized Hazel's house was sitting in a prime location. Seated on the edge of the bluff overlooking Lake Michigan, you could see nearly two towns away—almost 10 miles! The sidewalk leading up to the door, was also surrounded by an array of colorful flowers, as were the sides of the house and the perimeter of the garage.

"I wish I could do this around my house," I thought, as I rang the bell.

I was welcomed at the door by an excited little black and white Shih Tzu named Bella. Bella was Hazel's baby and very spoiled. Hazel wouldn't go anywhere without Bella, who stuck to Hazel like glue.

Once inside, I found Hazel and her son Bob to both be very pleasant. I also quickly noticed that Hazel looked rather young for 96. It was apparent that she had taken good care of herself over the years and was very particular about her appearance. She had short grey hair that appeared to be freshly permed. Her outfit, a light blue top with black slacks, reminded me of what my grandma wore to church. Her jewelry and makeup complimented her outfit and to top it all off, she had a kind smile—one that you just knew was genuine. We talked for a bit about the particulars of the job, but overall, it didn't take long for all three of us to feel comfortable with one another. By the time I left a relatively short time later, it was decided that I would stay with Hazel on an occasional, as-needed basis from 10 p.m-7a.m. Perfect!

I spent my first night at Hazel's on August 6th. Things went like clockwork. After putting the kids to bed, my husband and I had a little time together before I left. He would be there with the kids all night, and I would be home before they were even up (most of the time) the next morning. At Hazel's, I was able to catch up on some reading and much needed sleep, which was nice, considering both of those are rare commodities when you are the mom of two small children. I mean, think about it—how many people do you know that get to sleep on the job? So again, I say, "I couldn't have asked for anything better!".

Chapter 3: Unwanted Visitors

When someone actually takes the time to look back over their life, the fact of the matter is that we will be able to recall a relatively small number of events and circumstances in *great* or *finite* detail. Only a small number will be etched into our hearts and minds like the scar that never completely fades away. Few will be so deeply engraved that even the most mundane and insignificant details can be recalled with precision. For me, Halloween, October 31, 2010 is one of those events.

The evening started at my grandma's house. The kids and I had stopped to visit her after a long evening of trick-or-treating. I can still picture my then three-year-old son, Caleb as if it were yesterday. He was sitting on the living room floor with his face covered in chocolate as he scrounged through his bag of goodies. He still had his Spiderman costume on—except for the mask. My daughter Hailey, who was eighteen months old at the time, was sprawled on the floor sound asleep in her ladybug costume. I glanced up at my grandma's Grandfather clock as it chimed once to signify half past the hour. It was 8:30 p.m., which meant I needed to leave and get my kids home to bed because I was scheduled to be at Hazel's by 10:00 p.m.

When I got to Hazel's she was sitting in her favorite blue lazy boy recliner in the living room already in pajamas. When I walked into the room I could tell by the look in her eyes that she was tired—so tired that her smile was somewhat forced. She had been patiently waiting for me to arrive; anxious to lock the doors and go to bed. We briefly exchanged hello's and recounted the events of our day to one another.

Minutes later, I helped her get settled into bed and wished her goodnight. I glanced down at Bella and grinned. She was curled up in her usual spot at Hazel's feet, and Hazel had covered her up with a little blanket…as usual.

As I left the room, I placed Hazel's child safety gate in front of the door. The gate wasn't for her. It was for Bella. Hazel was worried Bella would get up in the night and leave the room. I don't think there's anything that could have caused Bella to leave Hazel's side, but if it gave Hazel peace of mind, then so be it. It was a small thing to ask and I was more than happy to oblige.

After Hazel and Bella were all tucked in for the evening, I went into my room, which was right next to Hazel's, got myself ready for bed, and snuggled in with a good book. It didn't take long for me to drift off to sleep, and before I knew it, the alarm was sounding. It was 6:30

a.m.—time for me to make my bed and head to the kitchen to start the coffee.

But wait a minute—what was *that* doing in here? The 'that' I was looking at, was the child gate I had clamped into place in the doorway of Hazel's room the night before. What was it doing here, propped up against the china cabinet a few feet from where I was standing? And how did it get there? I knew that Hazel couldn't have moved it. She used a walker, and I would have heard her if she tried. I stood there for a moment trying to sort it out but gave up and went on with my morning tasks so I could get home on time. After all, stranger things had happened, right? I just didn't know how much stranger…more frightening…more *terrifying* things could get.

My next night at Hazel's started out like all the others had, but I was startled out of my sleep when the phone rang. I sleepily looked at the clock. It was 2:30 a.m.! "Who would be calling this early?" It only rang once, so I decided it was probably some drunk person calling the wrong number. Slightly annoyed, I rolled over and went back to sleep until the alarm went off at 6:30.

The next several nights I spent at Hazel's 'treated me' to a repeat performance. Every night, my phone rang around 2:30-2:45 a.m. And every night, I woke up startled.

After a few nights of this, I knew this wasn't some drunk dialing the wrong number. Someone was prank calling us and enjoying it. But who would do that, and why? I decided to ask Mary, who also spent occasional nights at Hazels, if the same thing happened to her. She said that yes, it happened occasionally, but contributed it to a fluke with the phone company or phone towers. She also suggested that if it happened again, maybe we should contact them about it.

I agreed and assumed that the mystery of the unknown caller was solved. The next night I spent at Hazel's, though, proved me wrong. Terribly wrong.

Right on schedule, the phone rang again in the middle of the night, but this time, I also heard voices outside my room, in the kitchen, and in the living room area. I froze! I was too scared to move or say anything.

All I could think about was how they even got inside. I was certain I had locked all the doors before going to bed. But it sounded like there was a houseful of people on the other side of my bedroom door. I strained to make out their words but couldn't. Then suddenly it hit me that maybe they weren't real people—that they were ghosts.

Seriously? Did I just think that? But what other explanation could there be? Even if someone had broken into the house, there wouldn't have been that many of them, and they certainly wouldn't be making that much noise, so....

Terrified, I locked my gaze on the bedroom door. With eyes as wide as saucers, I stared intently into the darkness; trying to get a glimpse of something. Anything! I knew that the dome light above the stove in the kitchen was on. Out of habit, I always turned it on before going to bed in case I had to get up to help Hazel during the night. I was hoping that it would help me see something, but it didn't.

Seconds after that, my mind started racing frantically in circles in search of a more logical...realistic explanation. I sat up in my bed and tried to breathe without making a sound. I did not want to alert the intruders in any way. If I could have, I would have laughed to myself over that one, because I am quite sure anyone could have heard my heart beating violently in my chest. As hard and fast as it was pounding, it's a wonder it didn't explode.

I wasn't coming up with any plausible explanation, and with every passing second, I became more frightened over the possibility of them (whoever 'them' was) coming into my room. What would I do? I was completely and utterly alone. Since I hadn't heard Hazel call out, I was sure she was still sound asleep. But it wasn't like she would have been able to help, anyway, and I wasn't completely sure I had it in me to brave what was on the other side of the door, so yes, it was most definitely better that she not wake up.

The voices continued for what seemed like forever. In reality, it was a little over two hours—which in 'scared out of my wit's time—is almost an eternity. But finally, a little before 5, the voices stopped, fatigue and stress took over, and I actually drifted off to sleep.

When the alarm sounded at 6:30 a.m., it jolted me out of a not-so-sound sleep. I laid in bed for a minute listening for the voices. As I did, I looked around my room to see if anything was amiss. Nothing. In fact, the sun starting to come up and peeking through my windows was peaceful and calming.

I couldn't deny I'd had a rough night of it, and that *something* strange had happened. But I was still here and unharmed, so I needed to get on with the morning's tasks so I could get home to my family. I knew there had to be a logical explanation for what had happened. "There has to be!" I said to myself a few times. I also thought that maybe, some of the other girls that help take care of Hazel had decided to play a prank on me. That thought passed rather quickly, though, because it just wasn't something any of them would do.

When I left my room, I could see for myself that everything was in place and that there was no sign of any sort of commotion or 'going's on'. I shook my head in disbelief and did my best to go about the normal routine so that Hazel wouldn't see I was upset.

I continued to work nights at Hazel's even though I am not the least bit ashamed to say I was scared—especially when it came time to go to bed.

After 'that night', similar incidents happened once in a while for a few weeks. Then they started happening every night I was there, and it began to be more than 'just' voices in the house. One instance involved Hazel's Life Alert bracelet. If help was needed, all she had to do was push the button. A device in the guest room would then notify the hospital to send an ambulance. Some nights the life alert machine would go off at the same time as the phone. In a panic, I would jump out of bed and race into Hazel's room to find her sound asleep. I expected the ambulance to show up at her house, but it never did; making it apparent they never received the call.

Next, other girls started complaining about the phone and the life alert machine going off in the middle of the night. I have to admit I was somewhat relieved to know I wasn't the only one dealing with this. It also put my mind at ease about the possibility that I was 'losing it'. After comparing notes, we had a technician come out to replace the device. Installing the new device, however, did not correct the problem.

One night I was lying in bed reading a book. It was rather late, but I was having trouble going to sleep. Go figure, right! Hazel was thankfully sleeping soundly in the room next to mine, with Bella faithfully curled up next to her feet as usual. The house had been silent for several hours, but suddenly the silence was broken by a low rumbling sound that seemed to spread like a wave throughout the walls and ceiling. It was followed by some banging and louder rumbling sounds as if the pressure were building up in the pipes inside the walls. Growing up in old houses, I was used to hearing normal noises throughout the night such as a furnace or fridge kicking on, but the water running through the pipes was louder than normal. You could just about feel the sound vibrate as if there was a volume knob and somebody decided to crank it to max!

Then just like that, the rumbling stopped. The rumbling was replaced by the sound of running water. I could hear water…lots and lots of water gushing. It was so loud I knew beyond a doubt that the house was being flooded. But that was not the case.

I got out of bed and went into the kitchen and living room area. Nothing. "Where is it going?" I asked myself. "The basement!" But there was no way I was going to the basement to check things out. I was too scared. I decided if the basement flooded, we'd let the professionals deal with it. Instead, I checked to make sure Hazel was still sleeping, which she was, and went back to my room to wait for it to stop...like all the other strange things did. Finally, after a couple of hours, silence came, and I was able to get a few hours of restless sleep.

FYI: I later found out the basement was bone dry. The whereabouts of the water...who knows?

Another night I was in bed reading, when suddenly a foul odor permeated the air. The best way to describe it is to say it smelled like the dirty rooms in hospitals and nursing homes. It came on suddenly and was pretty intense, but slowly the smell faded away.

On more than one occasion I felt the weight of something or someone sitting on my stomach while I was lying in bed. Can you imagine?! If not, let me help you out. You are lying in bed reading or even sleeping, when suddenly you feel pressure on your stomach as if someone had just plopped down to sit on you. You look, but nobody is there. You want to think you are imagining it, but you can feel them, and you can't make the feeling go away.

Each time it feels like one of my kids has plopped down on my stomach (about 30 pounds worth). I tried to push it off once, but whenever I would push 'on' it, I was pushing through thin air, yet the pressure of the weight was still there. After about 15 minutes or so, it always left just as quickly as it came. Each time it happened I had what I call a mental heart attack. There was no way this stuff was normal. Honestly, though, at that point, I wasn't sure I knew what normal was anymore. All I knew was that I was scared out of my wits and didn't know what to do.

Another unsettling incident took place when I was roused out of my sleep by a male voice coming from the left side of my bed. As strange as it may sound, I wasn't all that frightened. I think I was too exhausted to be scared. Too tired to care that I could feel the presence of the man beside my bed, yet not see him. He repeated a sentence to me three times, but he was speaking in a foreign language, so I couldn't understand what he was saying. I sensed from the tone of urgency in his voice, though, that he was trying to give me some sort of directions. The urgency in his voice caused me to go from exhausted ambivalence to fearful angst and, made me fully awake. When I was fully awake and shaking with fright, he immediately left.

Chapter 4: Too Much to Handle

The situation at Hazel's only intensified until I could hardly handle it. I worried constantly about having to go there. My anxiety level grew as my time got closer to go there. What made it even more difficult was the fact that I was afraid to discuss my experiences with anyone. After the first couple of incidents I confided in my husband and mother-in-law, but they didn't believe me. They said I was just dreaming.

"I know for a fact I was awake!" I protested adamantly, but the look on their faces told me everything. Grinning at each other and trying not to laugh--they thought it was all a big joke!

Their indifference was both frustrating and hurtful. And when it became obvious that both my husband and mother-in law were tired of hearing about my experiences, I quit talking to them. So, think about that for a moment. If the love of your life and the mother in-law you love and trust don't believe you, who else was there? If the two people I trusted most didn't trust me to be telling the truth, why would anyone else? My answer to that was 'no one', which left me very much alone and scared with absolutely no one to confide in or draw courage and encouragement from.

Then one day, feeling particularly desperate for affirmation, I decided to ask Beth, one of the other girls who stayed with Hazel, if anything weird ever happened when she was there. I tried to word my question carefully, so she didn't think I was crazy. And yes, I admit that in light of my husband and mother in-law's attitudes, I asked myself if maybe I was crazy. I asked myself, "Do crazy people know if they are crazy?" But my head, my gut, and my heart knew better. I was not crazy, and I was not imagining anything. And praise God, Beth's answers to my question confirmed that

Beth nervously told me about the walking and talking she heard at night and the water in the pipes gushing so loud she thought the basement was flooding. She had also seen a guy walking around outside by the trees in the middle of the night that slowly faded away. She also said that one night, the two touch lamps on either side of her bed in the guest room blinked on and off by themselves.

Beth's experiences were nearly identical to mine! I was both relieved and scared that this was the case. It was comforting to know that I was no longer alone and that I was in fact not crazy. But one thing did bother me, though. It was the way Beth talked about it all. She spoke as if these things were a normal part of life. Her face showed no sign of fear, she didn't shake, and her voice did not crack. Why? Was Beth brave, which made me a big chicken?

At this point I'm sure you are wondering why I was still working at Hazel's. If I was so scared and these things really were happening, why did I put myself through it? The answer is money. I was desperate for the extra money. At this point my husband had been unemployed for a while, so as the saying goes, desperate people sometimes do desperate things

I couldn't get over the fact that Beth was so calm about it all. But as we continued talking I came to learn why. She had been having similar experiences her entire life. She said that in the beginning she was afraid—like I am. She said that after a while, though, she just accepted it. She believes that the ghosts were Hazel's family members trying to comfort her before she dies and goes to Heaven. She told me not to be afraid because they were not there for me. She also said that she usually told them to leave her alone—to go to Hazel. And more often than not, she said they did.

I didn't know whether to be impressed or taken

aback by her attitude. She was so comfortable with them that she talked to them…and they listened! Talking to Beth also gave me a sense of relief and resignation—especially when she told me that she'd heard one of them speak one night.

"It was muffled," she said, "But I am positive I heard one of them call for Bobby."

Bob, remember, is Hazel's son. And Beth thought it was the man's voice that spoke, so she felt certain it was Hazel's husband Roy, who passed away in 1981.

Beth's matter of fact attitude gave me a little boost of bravery. I continued to work at Hazel's and tried to accept the fact that the ghostly visitors were who and what Beth said they were—angels from Heaven sent to watch over Hazel. I continued telling myself that I shouldn't be afraid, but as hard as I tried, I failed. I couldn't convince myself that Beth was right, and I was still very much afraid.

One night, however, I'd been exceptionally busy at Hazel's, so when I went to bed, I was so exhausted that I slept the entire night. When my alarm went off, I was pleasantly relieved that I had made it through the night without having to experience another 'incident'. I got up feeling rested and ready to take on the day, so I got dressed and quickly began doing my usual morning tasks before

Mary, Hazel's next caregiver arrived.

At one point I glanced out the window just in time to see Mary through the garage window putting her car away. She had two other ladies with her that I didn't know. At first, I assumed they were dropping her off. I then realized that probably wasn't the case since she was putting her car in the garage. There was a heavy-set lady that was about 5' 2'' tall with straight blond hair to her chin. She was talking and laughing. The other lady was taller. I was unable to see her face because her back was to me, but she had brown hair with a bunch of tiny curls. When the blond lady started to walk out of the garage, I headed for the back door to let them in.

Mary walked in by herself. I was confused and asked Mary if someone had dropped her off. Now it was her turn to look confused. She shook her head and said, "No, I just put my car in the garage."

In that moment I then knew that the ladies I saw were not real. My heart began to race. Mary didn't have a clue that two women had been talking and laughing within a few inches of her! I decided, however, not to say anything to her. I just wanted to get out of there and go home. After telling Hazel goodbye, I literally ran past the garage to my car parked out front. After checking the backseat to make sure they weren't in there, I sped off and headed for home.

Ten minutes later I pulled into our driveway, walked in the door, and found my husband standing in the kitchen making breakfast; bacon and eggs

"I am never going back there ever again!" I boldly announced, slamming the door behind me. With my entire body shaking and my voice cracking, I told my husband what happened at Hazels. Just as I expected, he didn't believe me. I knew he was angry because we needed the money, but I didn't care. I finally decided that I had enough and there was no way he was going to change my mind.

I was afraid of my own shadow and every little noise the rest of the day. The two ladies I saw looked as real as could be. "Maybe I have seen ghosts out in public before and didn't know it?" I thought to myself. After what I saw that morning, I can honestly say that it would be hard to tell the difference. I was also so scared that the ghosts were going to visit *me* that I stayed up until 4:30 a.m. worrying about it.

When my husband saw how terrified I was and how deeply it was affecting me, he *finally* conceded that I might actually be telling the truth. Plus, every time he brought up the subject about going back to Hazel's, I would get angry and burst into tears. He knew I wasn't the sort of person to run from responsibility or my problems, so finally he realized this was more than just a problem. This was something bigger. Much bigger.

Chapter 5: Trudging Along

It took me a couple of days to be able to take a deep breath without it catching in my throat and to stop jumping out of my skin at every little movement and noise. It also took me that long to work up the nerve to call Pam, the lady who made out the schedule at Hazel's, to tell her why I would have to quit.

Pam also happened to be Kimberly's mom. Kimberly, as in my childhood BFF who had given me the opportunity to work for Hazel in the first place. Pam had known me most of my life, which is why I knew I could be honest with her about why I was quitting. I was certain she would believe me and not make me feel like I was crazy or trying to come up with the excuse of the century to get out of a job.

I was certain because…well, because this wouldn't be our first conversation about things like this. Pam, Kimberly, and their entire family had experienced similar incidents over the years and had been open with me about them. I knew they were true, because sometimes when I spent the night at their house as a kid, I also heard ghosts talking and walking around in their house.

And then there were those other times…

Like the time I was babysitting a little boy in a house across the street from us. I showed up at his house at 1:30 in the afternoon. His mom was getting ready to leave and the little boy chased a kitten up their stairs (there was a door to the upstairs and they never used it unless they had family stay from out of town.) I followed the boy and the kitten upstairs. There was a bunch of old furniture in the room. I felt like someone was watching me. Of course there was no one in there, but I couldn't shake the feeling, so I tried to find the kitten as fast as I could and get myself, the kitten, and the little boy back downstairs.

Later that night, I was watching an old Tom Cruise movie in the living room. The kitten was asleep on my lap and the little boy was asleep in his bed. Suddenly I heard a bunch of voices coming from the upstairs. I went to check on the little boy to make sure he wasn't the one talking. He was sound asleep. I walked through the downstairs of the house and looked in the garage. Nothing there. So, I went to back to the living room and tried to focus on my movie. But I was completely terrified…and still hearing voices.

I was tempted to take the little boy out of his bed and run across the street to my house, but before I could get the nerve up to do that, his parents came home. I did not say a word to them or my own parents for fear that they would think I was crazy or too immature to babysit.

And then there were the times I used to wake up in the middle of the night at my own house and see the light on in that upstairs room in the house across the street (the one I babysat at). It would blink on and off—even when the rest of the house was completely dark.

These are just a couple of examples of incidents I experienced over the years. I was pretty young, and it was so traumatic that I blocked them out of my memory for years. But when things started happening at Hazel's, it all came flooding back.

So, when I started talking to Pam, all I could think was, "Wow! I can't believe I actually 'said' that out loud." I've kept it all locked away for so long. I never even told my parents about it until just recently. But it's true. The incidents at Hazel's house were unnerving and terrifying, I'd never doubted they were real because of what had happened years ago.

Telling Pam was like lifting a weight off my chest. She didn't think I was crazy at all. In fact, Pam was also having experiences at Hazel's and said it was a relief to be able to talk to someone about it who understood where I was coming from…someone who believed me.

Besides hearing voices and seeing shadows, Pam once felt someone breathe on her and grab her neck. I couldn't even begin to imagine what my response to that would have been…and I didn't ever want to find out! On another occasion, she said a ghost was playing with candy wrappers on the nightstand beside her bed. But just like Beth, Pam wasn't overly scared. She believed the ghosts were Hazel's family members. Completely harmless. She also told me she knew Hazel would not want to lose me, so she would be happy to switch me to the day shift, and would I please take a couple of days to think it over.

Since we needed the money I forced myself to give the day shift a try. The day shift was 7 a.m.-2 p.m., which meant it was still dark outside for the first hour I was there. Knowing how scared I was, and why, Beth kindly offered to stay with me a couple times until it got light outside. We would sit quietly in the living room and talk while Hazel was still sleeping. Beth told me stories of her sleeping at her Grandpa's house as a young girl and witnessing her deceased Grandma visit her Grandpa on a regular basis. She even admitted getting an occasional visit from a deceased family member now and then. That's why none of this bothered her, she said.

Since she was so comfortable in talking about it, and since she seemed to be somewhat knowledgeable on the subject, I asked Beth if she knew why Mary was unable to see the two ladies that were with her, but I could. She said she believes that some people are more close-minded than others about things like that and that the spirits can tell who is open to experiencing them and who isn't. She made it sound like the people who are open to these experiences stand out to these ghosts or spirits like a porch light on a dark, snowy night. She also said that she believes that a person's ability to experience these things varies from person to person—that the more open you are, the more you will experience, but that if someone wants a deeper relationship or interaction with them, they can. They just have to 'practice' being more accessible.

I couldn't believe how nonchalant she was about it. I also couldn't believe someone would actually want to deal with this stuff. One thing was 'off' though, in what she said. The part about being open to the experiences making them more frequent. I didn't want *any* experiences. I wished it had never happened and that it would never happen to me again. And I told her so. I told her that I didn't want any part of it, but that I didn't seem to have a choice. Beth just smiled, assured me that I had nothing to be afraid of, and went on to talk about something else as if our conversation were completely normal.

Me? I sighed, wished it was a conversation I didn't have to have, and hoped that the glimmer of reassurance she'd given me stuck around for a long time. Or that the spirits didn't.

Over the course of the next few weeks and months, other girls that worked at Hazel's began sharing their ghostly experiences with me. I have to admit it was nice to have other people to empathize with. At least now I didn't feel so alone. Or worry that maybe I really was losing my mind. Mary was the exception and told us we were all nuts. Every time she made a comment like that, I was glad all over again that I hadn't said anything to her. Or that she wasn't the first person I'd gone to. Oh, and another thing…it appeared that most of these experiences happened at night. That means for day shift girls like me, incidents were fewer and farther between. Except for…

The times I would hear strange voices, see shadows of people who weren't there, lights would blink on and off, doors would slam shut, and this air of negativity and unrest that would sometimes just 'come' and hang in the room like someone were throwing a towel over your head. Some of the girls told me Hazel would tell them about her sisters and husband coming to visit her. One evening Hazel refused to go to bed because she claimed that her husband was sitting on the couch and they were having a conversation!

Even if I didn't notice their presence, Bella would become restless when ghosts were around. She seemed to watch them and would sometimes growl. Even Hazel and a couple of the other girls noticed her dog's odd behavior.

"What's wrong Bella? What are you looking at?" Hazel would ask several times as if she expected an answer.

I knew what was wrong. Knowing there was someone in the room I could not see sent chills up my spine. Not wanting to discuss my thoughts with Hazel, I would cringe and silently say to myself, "Yes, Bella, what exactly do you see?"

We, as in us girls, weren't the only ones dealing with all of this. Gary, the guy who took care of Hazel's yard, encountered these spirits…beings…or whatever you want to call them. He told us that it wasn't uncommon for him to feel as if someone was watching him whenever he took equipment out of the shed or garage.

Hearing him talk about the garage always reminded

me of the two ladies I saw with Mary. I hadn't stepped foot in the garage since then, nor would I ever do so again. No way! I'm sure Hazel wondered why I didn't take her up on her offer to let us use the garage—especially in the winter. She never asked me about it, but even if she would have, I would have said, "No thanks!" I would scrape frost, ice, and snow off the windshield without complaining before I would park in there.

At some point I also learned from Pam that the ghost ladies I saw in the garage may have been Hazel's sisters. My description of the ladies resembled pictures she has seen of them. The blonde lady I saw looked to be around 30 years old, so since I had only seen pictures of Hazel's sisters when they were much older, I couldn't tell for sure. I was told I might be able to find younger pictures of her sisters in the basement, that would provide a more positive ID, but I was too afraid to go down there and look for them. I wasn't really even sure I wanted to know.

Working the day shift was less stressful than working the night shift, and we really did need the money, so that's what I did for quite some time. Several months, in fact. But I made it clear to Pam that I would quit before I would ever work a night shift again. Of course I saw the night shift girls when I came to relieve them, and they would tell me about all the bazar and frightening things they encountered. I felt sorry for them, of course, because I knew what that fear felt like. Thankfully, though, the encounters I had during the day were less frightening. Partly because it was daylight, and partly because the nature of these 'visits' was less intimidating and 'dark'. They were more 'casual'—if that makes sense.

  The word casual is the last word I would have ever imagined myself using in the same breath as words like 'ghost' and 'spirits', but that was my life. For better or worse (definitely worse), that was my life.

Chapter 6: Bob's Visit

The following April, which meant I'd been working at Hazel's for over six months, Hazel's son Bob and his wife Lisa came from California for a surprise visit. Hazel was thrilled. Most of her family lived out of the area, including her daughter, Jackie, who lived in Battle Creek, Michigan. Don't get me wrong—both Bob and Jackie were loving and respectful toward Hazel and did their best to make sure she had everything she needed. Both of them also took every possible opportunity to visit their mom, but it wasn't as often as Hazel hoped. She understood why they couldn't come more often, but as a mom, and being elderly, having them around was a delightful 'treat' and break from the reality of her life. A life that consisted of sitting around in her big, fine house with caregivers, a yard man, her beloved dog, Bella, and a bunch of ghosts.

Another plus for the night shift girls, was that when Bob or Jackie visited, they got time off because her family was there to see to her needs.

Bob and Jackie did, ask, however, that those of us who worked during the day would still come to take care of meals, and the other regular duties. They weren't familiar with what needed to be done, so rather than upset Hazel's routine, they preferred for us to be there.

One morning when I arrived at Hazel's, she was still sleeping. "Can I talk to you for a minute in the sunroom?" Bob whispered. "Sure," I replied. Hazel took pride in her sunroom. I can still picture her telling me, "It wasn't always a sunroom, you know? It used to be an outdoor patio, but I had it enclosed to keep the bugs out." She would tell me about the numerous get-togethers she had in there with friends throughout the years. Even though she didn't use it as much anymore, she always kept it nice. It was one of my favorite spots in the house, too.

I followed Bob into the sunroom, and we sat down across from each other around the glass table. "So, how is everything going here?" Bob asked. It was obvious he was trying to figure out how to get to the real point of the conversation without just blurting it out.

"It is going really good," I answered. There was no way I was going to tell him about the ghostly experiences. I needed this job, and now that I was strictly days, it was going well. Without really realizing what was happening, I was becoming almost as ambivalent to the ghosts as Pam and Beth were. Besides, there was no way I was going to give him any cause for concern that a crazy lady was helping his mother!

"That's good to know," Bob said slowly, "but my mother has been telling me that my dad has been coming to visit her quite frequently. I want to assume that these 'visits' are a part of her dementia. My father has been deceased for quite some time, you know," he said.

I nodded politely. I could tell by the look in his eyes, though, that he was looking for something more. That he no longer believed dementia was the answer to his questions.

Finally, after a few seconds of awkward silence, he asked, "Have you experienced anything unusual?"

I shifted nervously in my chair for a few seconds trying to decide what to say and do. I had never been one to lie. I believe that the truth is always the best answer. The only right answer. Taking a deep breath and looking around thinking this would be my last time in this house, I decided to give him the truth and said, "I don't think your mom is imagining anything."

Bob almost looked relieved. The look of relief was quickly replaced by one that said, "I'm curious. I want to know more. I *need* to know more. So I gave him more. For the next several minutes I proceeded to tell him everything. Unsure of how he was going to react, I was relieved when he thanked me.

"What you have experienced is very special," he said.

Special isn't the word I would use to explain it, but as long as I wasn't going to lose my job, he could call it whatever he wanted. Bob followed his 'special' comment by telling me that he and his wife had seen shadows walk around and had other experiences as well. "I don't recall any of this going on when I came to visit last October," Bob said. "Can you tell me when it started?"

"It all started the last weekend of October," I answered.

As we continued to talk, I learned that Bob's father used to call him 'Bobby' when he was a child. This confirmed that the voice Beth heard saying "Bobby" was probably his dad. Bob also told me that he didn't want any of us (meaning Hazel's caregivers) to discuss our experiences with her. I told him that was fine; that we hadn't done so, nor did we have any intention of doing so in the future. He did say, however, that if his mother talked to us about things, he would like us to listen attentively. Like Beth, Bob believed that the ghosts at Hazel's were members of their family sent by God to help her before she died.

Chapter 7: Searching for Answers

I thought about my experiences at Hazel's regularly. Okay, so I was borderline obsessed by them. I tried to convince myself that Bob and Beth were right—that the ghosts at Hazel's were her family members, sent by God to help her before she died. "If God wants to send deceased family members to comfort us before we die then I guess He can," I thought.

I tried. I really tried to buy off on this, but I just couldn't. I couldn't shake the feeling…the conviction planted deep in my heart and mind, that the spirits at Hazel's were intentionally trying to scare us. And as far as I knew, this was not something God would approve of—much less participate in.

I tried talking about this with my close friends and family members to get their opinion. Even though they were great listeners, they didn't have any answers for me. How could they? They still weren't convinced it was even true.

When my family was sound asleep at night, I would stay up late searching for answers on the computer. I came across a lot of material, but I didn't feel good about looking at a lot of it. You could tell just by looking at the images on the screen and the opening statements that a lot of these websites were dark. Evil. Satan-sanctioned. Meant to pull us away from God.

As a Christian, I was raised knowing that God does not approve of psychics and witchcraft. The Bible clearly calls these things sinful.

Now before I go any farther in telling you my story, I want to take a few minutes to let you know where I am in matters of faith. To begin, I want to say that I have purposely waited until now to do so. That might make some of you question my faith and the legitimacy of my relationship with God but hear me out before you decide. First of all, I did pray. A lot. I wasn't trying to do this on my own. For every question I asked Beth and Pam, I asked God a hundred more. I prayed the words of one of my favorite Psalms more times than I can count.

When I am afraid I will trust in you; in God whose word I praise. ~Psalm 56:3-4 NIV

But quite honestly, when the incidents didn't stop, I had a few doubts. I didn't understand why God was not helping me.

It took me a while (longer than I really care to admit) for me to see getting to move to the day shift was an answer to my prayers. I needed the job but was unable to handle the terrors that were coming in the night, so God answered my prayers by moving me to the day shift. It also took a while (a lot longer) to see God's faithfulness to me in all of this and his reasons for calling me to be a witness and testimony of the realities of Satan in this world and what he and his demons are capable of.

Another reason I wasn't very vocal about my faith through all of this is the reason I'll call skepticism and self-consciousness. My reasoning was that if my husband, who loved and cherished me above all others, and my mother in-law, who I have a great relationship with, didn't believe me, then what would the preacher say? How would he respond? Would he think I was demon possessed and not allow me in church? Would he think I was trying to cause strife and division in the church? Would he think I was crazy? Would he think I was looking for attention? Was there even the slightest chance he would believe me? And if so, what would, or could he do?
All those questions and the answers I gave myself to each of them, are why I decided to wrestle this with God privately. I could feel God's presence in my heart and

mind. Recognizing and welcoming God's presence is why I was so frightened…terrified of what was happening. I know that now—that the intense fear was God's way of protecting me from getting sucked into the complacency and accepting attitude most of the other girls had. So, instead of delving into the darkness of most of the websites I found, I sought out Christian websites that addressed the issue. I also decided to find a pastor who didn't know me, but that I would feel comfortable and safe going to for answers and guidance.

    I'd made an appointment to talk to the pastor at our church, but when I told him just a snippet of what I wanted to meet with him about, I immediately heard the hesitation in his voice. I ended up cancelling the meeting because he decided we needed witnesses there, too. I just couldn't shake the feeling that the meeting would end up being fodder for the fellowship times after Bible study. Or that I would become the church's 'project'.

    I know that sounds bad—like the church is full of a bunch of gossiping old biddies, but that's not what I'm saying. I'm just saying that the potential is there for the meeting to turn into a very public debate. That was the last thing I wanted or needed, so my search for a pastor was on.

The pastor I found didn't discount my feelings or make me feel like I was demon possessed or some kind of heathen. He stressed the importance of the Bible; getting to know what it says and holding on to each word as my anchor of truth. I am forever grateful for his patience and his help, even though it took a while for me to see just how helpful he really was. And as you will read later on, his Godly patience and discipling was instrumental in my journey toward realizing the hope and power that comes when you give your life to the Lord.

My determination to seek God's truth and apply it to my life paid off one night when I came across a Christian website. Its primary message was to warn Christians and non-Christians alike to stay away from familiar spirits. The website pointed out what God has to say in the Bible, which is what I wanted to know. To be reminded of. To hold on to with all my strength. Here are a few of the verses I found:

When someone tells you to consult mediums and spiritists, who whisper and mutter, should not a people inquire of their God? Why consult the dead on behalf of the living? ~Isaiah 8:19 NIV

Do not turn to mediums or seek out spiritists, for you will be defiled by them. I am the LORD your God.
~Leviticus 19:31 NIV

These Bible verses gave me the answer that I was searching for! What I was dealing with at Hazel's was not of God! The spirits appearing to Hazel as her husband and sisters were not really ghosts, but a demonic presence pretending to be them. Although I was thankful to discover the truth, it made me even afraid. I wasn't sure if it was a good idea for me to continue working at Hazel's at all. I constantly asked myself, "What powers do the evil spirits have? Could they possess me? Could they oppress me in some way?" I needed more answers.

Chapter 8: God is Very Real

After combing through the Christian website, I decided to talk to my mom's friend, Kris about my experiences at Hazel's and what I had learned about them online. I considered Kris to be a strong Christian woman, who was very knowledgeable when it came to the Bible. After listening intently, she said she didn't think it was a good idea to be around demonic activity at all—that it was giving Satan a toehold into your life. She read a couple of Bible verses to me to emphasize that this wasn't just her thoughts, but that they were God's Words...

Finally, be strong in the Lord and in his mighty power. Put on the full armor of God, so that you can take your stand against the devil's schemes. For our struggle is not against flesh and blood, but against the rulers, against the authorities, against the powers of this dark world and against the spiritual forces of evil in the heavenly realms. Therefore put on the full armor of God, so that when the day of evil comes, you may be able to stand your ground, and after you have done everything, to stand. Stand firm then, with the belt of truth buckled around your waist, with the breastplate of righteousness in place, and

with your feet fitted with the readiness that comes from the gospel of peace. In addition to all this, take up the shield of faith, with which you can extinguish all the flaming arrows of the evil one. Take the helmet of salvation and the sword of the Spirit, which is the word of God.
~Ephesians 6:10-17 NIV

Submit yourselves, then, to God. Resist the devil, and he will flee from you. ~James 4:7 NIV

And give no opportunity to the devil. ~Ephesians 4:27 ESV

I read these verses over and over again. I hadn't asked for any of this to happen. I didn't want any of this to happen. But at this point I had to ask myself if I was partly to blame because I didn't stand up to them; refusing to let them into my life.

    Kris agreed that talking to the pastor and his wife could help me. I called them and they agreed to meet with me the following Friday. My husband stayed home with the kids so that I could go to their house alone, which was a big deal to me, because even though he couldn't wrap his head around all of this, he was willing to support my efforts to make sense of it all and get help to make it stop. So, I left for their house, which is where we had agreed to meet, eagerly hoping, and praying for answers…and help. Before hearing my story, they said they wanted to know a little about my background and whether or not I was a Christian.

I told them that I knew that God sent his son Jesus Christ to die on the cross for our sins so that we can go to Heaven. I told them that when I was nine years old I asked Jesus to come into my heart and forgive me of my sins so that I might be saved. What I *didn't* tell them was what *kind* of Christian I was. A lukewarm…passive…mediocre one.

I've gone to church off and on with my family and have tried to be a 'good' person and do things that please God. I've always tried my best to be honest and kind. When I was in school I worked hard to get good grades and I never got into drinking or partying. So even though my parents raised me to know that the Bible tells us we are not saved by our good works, but by grace, I was trying to do just that—earn my salvation through being good. I had never learned to trust in God's promises enough to let them *be enough*. I had never developed a close, personal relationship with God.

I didn't even have a healthy prayer life, which says quite a bit considering everything going on in my life. As a kid and as a teenager, I was usually too busy with school, friends, work, and other things to make God a priority in my life. Then came marriage and the baby carriages (as the children's rhyme goes), to give me even more excuses not to make time for God. And I am ashamed to admit that even though I'd heard a lot of Bible stories growing up, I rarely read them for myself. I rarely picked up my Bible and had never read it in its entirety.

Sitting there telling that pastor and his wife in the vaguest terms possible what kind of Christian I was, was humbling and troubling. It wasn't easy to admit to myself that while I believed in God, I really didn't know him at all, and that the only times I made room for him was when I wanted or needed something.

What kind of Christian was I? I was barely one at all!

After I got through that, I told the pastor and his wife my story. The entire time I was talking, I looked for signs of disbelief on their faces, but there was none. When I finished talking, the pastor told me that he had similar experiences when he was younger and had also sought out answers. "Since you are a Christian, the demons will have a difficult time trying to possess you because God gives all Christians the authority to make evil spirits leave in his name," he said.

He also said I shouldn't fear them because the Bible says:

And these signs will accompany those who believe: In my name they will drive out demons; they will speak in new tongues. ~Mark 16:17 NIV

I now understand that while it is more difficult for a Christian to be demon possessed, it isn't impossible. God gives us all free will. So even if you become a Christian at some point in your life, if you don't live in faithful obedience, it is possible. If a person chooses sin over righteousness, it is always possible.

Getting back to my meeting with the pastor and his wife...

The pastor and his wife told me that when I go to Hazel's and something happens, I need to say firmly and resolutely, "Leave in the name of Jesus Christ!" The pastors wife went on to say that they had to listen, because even though Satan and his demons rule earth, God rules the universe Therefore, their rule is subject to his allowing it—which he will until the second coming of Christ.

I had my doubts about them 'having to leave',

because every time something happened, I would pray over and over for God to make them leave and he wouldn't. I told them I believe God has the power to make them leave, but I didn't understand why he didn't.

"Maybe he is allowing them to bother you so you will seek out the truth and to realize the power you have through the Holy Spirit," the pastor said. "Why should God do it for you, when you will grow more in tune and in love with him if *you* do it *through* him?"

What he said made a lot of sense. Since I had never read through the Bible before, I didn't know that. I was like someone trying to put something together without any instructions.

Next the pastor said something that blew my mind, but at the same time, was a huge relief and blessing. He said, "When you tell the spirits to leave, you must say it out loud. The devil doesn't have the ability to hear our thoughts or read our minds. He can only plant thoughts in our minds. In other words, he can only tempt us, but that's as far as he can go."

I told them I wasn't sure if I would be brave enough to stay at Hazel's another night, but if I ever did, I would do what they said. I could tell they were sincere, that they knew God's Word, and that they genuinely wanted to help.

Before I left, the pastor and his wife prayed with me…for me, really. It was the most amazing thing I have ever experienced. Three times throughout the prayer the pastor asked God to 'touch me.' Every time he said it, I felt an indescribable sensation throughout my body. It went from my head to my toes. It was a feeling no human being could give someone by touching them. Warm. Gentle. A little like something being poured over you, but yet all at once, too. God himself was touching me!!! I had never doubted God was real, but that night God became really real to me. More real than I could have imagined him every being in my life. I didn't even know it was possible to feel that close to God, but I was there, and I didn't want to leave—God, that is. I left the pastor's house with the faith I needed to stand up to the demons and cast them out in Jesus' name.

Chapter 9: A Test of Faith

In June, Hazel's son Bob and her daughter Jackie came to visit at the same time. I saw this as a great opportunity to talk to them about the spirits at their mother's house not being angels. I'm still not quite sure where I got up the nerve to do it, but somehow I did. I respectfully explained that one of Satan's favorite and most successful tactics is deception. He deceives people by making them believe his demons are God's angels. Unfortunately, I didn't have my Bible in hand to show them that the Bible says about this.

FYI: Not the best move on my part. But I'd come this far, so I told them, rather than showed them, what it said.

I said that even people sometimes disguise themselves as false prophets—workers for Christ, when in fact they are just the opposite. I told them that even, according to the Bible, disguises himself as an angel of light.

For such people are false apostles, deceitful workers, masquerading as apostles of Christ. And no wonder, for Satan himself masquerades as an angel of light. It is not surprising, then, if his servants also masquerade as servants of righteousness. Their end will be what their actions deserve. ~2nd Corinthians 11:13-15 NIV

Neither Bob nor Jackie was convinced that the situation was not God-honoring. They said they had a 'feeling' that the spirits residing in their mother's house were angels.

My response was, "If they are angels, then why are they trying to scare us?"

"It was the character of my mother's sisters to do that. If they were demons, they would probably be afraid of my mother because she has a mean streak," Jackie said jokingly.

Bob decided the conversation had gone far enough and said he didn't want the issue discussed anymore. Then later, when he found out that one of the ladies I worked with—one of his mom's caregivers—wanted a pastor to pray over the house, he was upset. "If I knew a pastor was going to pray over the house, I'd put a stop to it!" he insisted.

Their minds were made up, so we, as in those of us who worked for Hazel, had to deal with it on our own, in our own way, and not discuss it with either of them anymore. While I didn't agree with their methods of dealing with the situation, I had no intention of disrespecting them or overstepping my boundaries. But I was concerned for their mother.

It was one thing for them to believe the spirits were good, but believing the spirits are angels doesn't make it so. The Bible speaks the ultimate truth, and I knew without a doubt that they were not. At that moment, I realized how easy it is to be deceived and the importance of the Bible in our lives. It was one of those lightbulb in your head moments. The Bible truly is powerful. True. Real. The ultimate guide for living life the way it should be lived. It is, in the words of Paul in his second letter to Timothy…

All Scripture is God-breathed and is useful for teaching, rebuking, correcting and training in righteousness, so that the servant of God[a] may be thoroughly equipped for every good work.
~2nd Timothy 3:16-17 NIV

It is also the very thing the writer of the book of Hebrews says it is…

For the word of God is alive and active. Sharper than any

double-edged sword, it penetrates even to dividing soul and spirit, joints and marrow; it judges the thoughts and attitudes of the heart. ~Hebrews 4:12 NIV

Satan was pulling out all the stops, though. Basically, everyone at Hazel's thought the spirits were angels except for another lady and me. Even though we were scared, we felt it was important to get rid of the demons and agreed to cast them out in Jesus' name whenever we worked, and they chose to intrude on our lives.

It had been a while since I had spent the night at Hazel's, but I decided to give it another try. At the time, I was staying with her from 2-10 p.m. on Thursday and 6 a.m. to 2 p.m. on Friday. Since my kids were sleeping the short time, I was home, staying the night at Hazels made sense. They wouldn't even miss me.

I wish I could say that I had a lot of faith my first night back at Hazel's, but I didn't. I was so incredibly nervous. But I was also determined—determined to get ahead of the demons by stopping them before they even got started. So, when Hazel went into the bathroom to get ready for bed, I seized the moment to cast the demons out. Careful not to let Hazel hear, I quietly went into every room and said, "In the name of Jesus, leave!"

After I got Hazel and Bella settled into bed, I went into the guestroom to get myself settled for the night. Desiring a peaceful state of mind, but too tired to read, I browsed through a cookbook—something I enjoy doing. Before long I was nodding off and shortly after that, I was sound asleep. But like a little kid afraid of the dark, I intentionally left the light on.

Around 12:30 a.m., I woke up to something jumping on my legs. I assumed it was Hazel's dog Bella at first. Once I was more awake, I realized that wasn't possible, because Bella was with Hazel.

Fully awake, I turned to look at my legs and saw the imprints of two small feet on the white down blanket of my bed, doing a little dance. Fear engulfed me! The being was invisible, yet I could feel its weight—about fifteen pounds or so. Maybe even more. Almost too scared to speak, I managed to say, "In the name of Jesus leave!" I felt it leave immediately. Not just the weight, but the spirit or presence of doom, was gone, too.

Not leaving it open for discussion, so to speak, I told it to leave six more times. The absence I felt is hard to explain—it was physical as well as internal or spiritual.

I was relieved and thankful it was gone, But I was

also scared and angry. I began to cry. "Why did I ever agree to sleep here? I'm so stupid! Never again!"

Hazel was in the room next to mine, asleep and unaware that anything had happened. I also heard a big semitruck drive by on the highway. From the sound of his breaks as he descended the hill, I could tell he was carrying a heavy load. He wasn't the only one! I remember wishing that the driver had known what had happened and was turning around to save me. How silly is that, right!

Feeling utterly alone, I reached for my phone on the nightstand and called my husband. He had to get up for work in a few hours but agreed he would pray for me after we hung up. Next I called my friend Rietta. She and her husband Paul kindly prayed for me over the phone. After we hung up, I continued to pray on my own. I thanked God for helping me and asked him to protect me the rest of the night.

"God, please help me to be unafraid and give me the courage to stand up to these spirits that I know are not from you if they come back," I said.

Eventually I fell asleep again; waking up periodically, but each time I fell back asleep without any trouble, because every time I woke up, I heard a calm voice in my mind saying, "Everything is alright, go back to sleep." So, I did, and it was.

When my alarm went off, I offered up prayers of thanks to Jesus for his protection and assurance. I also thanked him for being the calm and loving Savior that he is. The peace he gives is so completely opposite of the feelings of dread and gloom that hover over you when Satan is near. I cannot even begin to comprehend why anyone would want that. Or why anyone would not run straight to Jesus after experiencing it.

I knew that since going to bed the night before that I had witnessed the dreadful power of Satan AND the great power of Jesus' name! And let me tell you, the power of Jesus is the power you want on your side.

Chapter 10: God Sends Reinforcement

Even though I knew the demons would leave in Jesus' name, I was worried that I had to have an encounter with them first in order to make them leave me alone. My imagination grew wild. "What if all of the demons in Hazel's house approached me at the same time," I thought. Would I be brave enough to speak if that happened!

I decided to talk to the pastor and his wife whom I had spoken with previously. I was hoping they could tell me how to make the demons leave for good. "You are doing everything right. But if it would make you feel better, I would be willing to go to Hazels and pray during the day if you would like," the Pastor said.

I thanked him for offering but knew that wasn't an option because of what Bob had said. I was just going to have to deal with them on my own as I had promised him, and Jackie I would. Besides, I didn't have to stay nights at Hazel's if I didn't want to, and don't think I didn't consider saying no all the time. A big part of me wanted to. But being fearful of the spirits in that house, I was growing closer to God and I was starting to grow as a Christian. I no longer considered it just a title or an affiliation. I had come to know it is who you are. A lifestyle, meaning it's how you live your whole life—not just something you do when it's convenient or appropriate.

Growing and maturing in my relationship with God was and always will be a wonderful thing, but with it comes the responsibility of living up to God's expectations and obeying his commands. So, I couldn't take the easy way out. I felt responsible as a Christian to get rid of the spirits. I knew God would never ask anything of me that he would not empower me to do, so I wasn't going to let him down.

One day I was browsing through the book section at Wal-Mart and came across a book called, *Prayers that Rout Demons & Break Curses*. Interested, I purchased it. I read through some of the prayers and found one that asked God to have his angels send the demons back to hell and lock them up there where they belong. The prayer also said something about asking God to have his angels form a protective hedge around the house (Eckhardt,62, 97-98). I decided that I would try to say a similar prayer the next night I spent at Hazel's. I figured that if God's angels sent the demons back to hell, then maybe I could get rid of them for good?

I realize there are things we don't fully know or understand about the details of Heaven and Hell as described in the book of Revelation (and other parts of the Bible, too). I also know that the prayers this book talked about may not be entirely 'on point' from a scriptural perspective. But what I did know in reading the book that the author was on God's side of things and that was a good thing. I believed (and still do) that God is more than okay with asking him to get rid of Satan's influence and interference in our lives and in asking for protection by his angles. I know this because the Bible tells us that God sends his angels to take care of us, protect us, and keep us from making choices we will regret.

Throughout this whole ordeal I have held on to verses like these to remind me that I am not alone—that I have God and his army of angels on my side.

For he will command his angels concerning you to guard you in all your ways. On their hands they will bear you up, lest you strike your foot against a stone.
~Psalm 91:11-12 NIV

Are they not all ministering spirits sent out to serve for the sake of those who are to inherit salvation?
~Hebrews 1:14 NIV

It was my third night back at Hazel's. I had just got her settled into bed and gone to my room to get ready for bed. I noticed that the screen windows in my room were open, so I closed them. It was hot outside, and the evening breeze would have been nice, but I didn't want to hear any noise that might scare me. I was already nervous. I didn't need anything else adding to my angst, so I climbed into my bed and started praying this prayer: *God, thank you for sending your son to die on the cross for our sins. Please forgive me for my sins. I want to get to know you better and live a life that is pleasing to you. Thank you for making the demons leave for me the last time I slept here. If they come here tonight, please give me the strength to make them leave in your name. Please send your angels to take the demons to hell and lock them up where they belong. Please send your angels to form a protective hedge around this house so nothing evil can get in. In your name I pray, Amen.*

As soon as I finished praying, I heard something with big wings flying outside the window behind my bed. I tried to think of a logical explanation and asked myself, "What flies around at night?" "Maybe a bat or an owl?"

No, it couldn't have been any of those. It was too loud, which meant it was too big to be either one. My next thought was that it wasn't a coincidence I had just finished asking God to send his angels to form a hedge of protection around the house. I had never seen an angel and wasn't sure if they actually had wings like I was hearing, but I decided to stay up and read my Bible for a little while. I figured as long as I was doing something that kept me close to God, I would be safe.

I fell asleep while reading my Bible and slept peacefully through the rest of the night. When I woke up, I knew that the harassment might not be over for good, but they couldn't hurt me since I had God on my side. God had once again kept his promise and shown me that his words are true by sending angels to protect me. I was both relieved and thankful beyond words!

All throughout the day I kept thinking about what I'd heard—the wings flapping. I knew it was angels flying; keeping watch over me. Something like this is too powerful not to share with someone you trust, so I told my brother and sister about it. Part of me was wanting their affirmation of my explanation. But to my disgrace, there was also a part of me still trying to explain things away in a more logical way, so I knew that if they didn't think it was angels, they would give me a 'normal' explanation I could accept. As it turns out, they were as convinced as I was that

God's angels had been sent to protect me from the demons. I apologized to God for doubting him and thanked him again for watching over me.

I want to press the pause button for a minute to share something about Hazel's place in all of this. They were at her house, so surely they felt…welcome? I didn't know, but once I started clinging to faith more than fear (or trying to, anyway). I felt I needed to talk to her about Jesus—to find out where she was in her relationship with him. Did she have one? Or was she aware that the demons felt free to take up residence in her home?

She told me numerous stories about her kids, owning a local grocery store, the times she spent in Florida over the winter and her memories of the Great Depression. But never did we talk about Jesus.

I remember one conversation we had one day after I asked her about a beautiful young lady in a picture hanging on her bedroom wall. I asked her who it was, and she said, "Me."

You could easily tell Hazel took great pride in her appearance when she was young. She still did. Even then when she was in her nineties, her daily attire consisted of a nice blouse and pleated dress pants. Her closet was full of dressy outfits. I often wondered if she had ever owned a pair of jeans. Her make-up and nails were always done, and she had her hair permed at the salon often.

Not only did she want her appearance to be immaculate, but her home and yard as well. Her lawn was always well kept in the summer with flowers beautifully adorning the landscape. In the winter, she wanted her sidewalk completely cleared and wanted you out there shoveling while it was still snowing. She even asked that I not walk through the snow in her yard but stay on the sidewalks.

She was definitely particular about things, but she had a big heart and was a sweet enjoyable person to be around. But again, as much as I thought I knew about Hazel I wasn't sure where she stood with God. She had been a devout Catholic and attended church religiously most of her life, but she couldn't get out of the house much at that point, so she watched mass on television. A priest from the local Catholic Church, where she was a member, also came to her house once a month to give her communion. So yes, she appeared to know God, but the fact that the demons were at her house really bothered me.

I knew that I should talk to her about God, but I just couldn't muster up the courage. I made excuse after excuse as to why 'this moment or that moment' was not the right time. Basically, I was arguing with God. Witnessing to someone was never easy for me. I kept putting it off until one night, when I did not have a choice. Hazel woke me up at 1:30 a.m. to tell me, "I think I am going to die tonight."

Hazel was ninety-seven years old at the time, so I knew the probability was pretty high, but I hoped I was not the one there when she did. "Why do you think that?" I asked. "I just feel very tired," she said. "Will you please take care of my dog if I go?" she asked.

I started to get nervous. I really hoped Hazel was going to be wrong about dying that night! My excuses had run out. That night I had no choice, but to face my fear and talk to Hazel about Jesus. So, I proceeded to do my best. We ended the night with a prayer and Hazel fell asleep two minutes later. Fortunately, Hazel was wrong, and we got to keep her a little while longer. In fact, we got to keep Hazel for another year. She died peacefully on June 27th, 2012 at the age of ninety-eight in a care home in Lower Michigan.

I remember praying that night after Hazel fell asleep. I told God I hoped I said the right things. I also worried that if I did say something wrong, it might have kept her from wanting to be saved…if she wasn't. I still didn't know for sure. That was one of the first times I had ever really talked to someone about Jesus and I hoped that I had done it correctly.

Chapter 11: The Afterlife

One day I was driving down the road with my three-year-old son when we drove past a small cemetery. Caleb pointed out the window at the multiple grave sites decorated with a various array of flowers and asked, "What's that Mommy?" He was at the age where he wanted to know about everything, and my daughter, who isn't much younger than he is, was quickly getting to the 'why' and 'what' stage, too. If you are a parent you know what I'm talking about. I couldn't make it through a single day without being asked dozens of questions. Don't get me wrong—I loved their curiosity, but sometimes I didn't know the answer or was unsure of how to word it in a way they could understand without confusing them or opening up the door to even more questions.

As I was trying to form the answer in my head about the cemetery, he impatiently asked again, "Mommy! What was that?"

"It is a cemetery and those are grave sites. When people die their bodies are buried in the ground and people put flowers on their grave to remember them," I replied.

I could tell by the look on his face in my rearview mirror that he was confused. We were already having regular talks about Jesus. He knew that when people die, some people go to Heaven and some people go to Hell.

"Mommy, some people go to Heaven to see Jesus and some people go to Hell to see the devil because he is naughty," he said.

"That's right," I replied.

"So why did they put those people in the ground?" he asked.

"Well when people die, their body gets buried in the ground, but they leave their body behind and go to Heaven or Hell," I said.

"But why do they put them in the ground?" he asked again.

I explained as simply as possible that when we die our bodies are no good to us anymore, so we put them in the ground to get rid of them. I know that may not have been the best way to word my response, but it was the best I could do at that moment. It was the best I could do because none of us really knows exactly what happens, how it happens, or when it happens. Only God knows the exact details of what happens after our death. The afterlife is a mystery to all of us, but through studying the Bible, we can learn what God wants us to know and that is all that matters.

For obvious reasons, this is something I've given a great deal of thought to. Not in trying to figure it all out, but more along the lines of trying to understand who or what the demons in Hazel's house are, and why they are there. I know there are countless books, websites, and 'experts' on the matter, but the Bible is the ultimate authority on all matters, so that is where I go for answers about the 'afterlife'.

From my own personal experience and in talking to others, the number-one question on everyone's mind is: Do we become angels, or can we watch over our loved ones after we die? The answer to that question, according to the Bible is: No, we don't, and no we cannot. The Bible tells us that when we die, we can't become a spirit that inhabits the earth again. Once we die, we are no longer able to think and converse with others here on earth. The Bible states:

For the living know that they will die, but the dead know nothing; they have no further reward, and even the memory of them is forgotten. Their love, their hate and their jealousy have long since vanished; never again will they have a part in anything that happens under the sun.
~Ecclesiastes 9:5-6 NLT

Whatever your hand finds to do, do it with all your might, for in the grave, where you are going, there is neither working nor planning nor knowledge nor wisdom.
~Ecclesiastes 9:10 NLT

When they breathe their last, they return to the earth, and all their plans die with them.
~Psalm 146:4 NLT

So, contrary to what Hazel's children and some of the other ladies who work with me believe, these spirits/demons were not hanging around to help ease Hazel from life to death or whatever in the afterlife. The goal of a demonic spirit is to taunt, torment, torture, tempt, and terrorize. The end. Angels, on the other hand, are protectors, helpers, encouragers, and news-bringers. They are forthright, humble, and there is nothing menacing about them. And people who die, are neither.

I have also heard people say shortly after the death of a loved one that they can still feel the presence of their loved one around and it comforts them. I feel for their loss and understand that they are grieving, but it worries me that they are being deceived. Not only is there loved one no longer there, meaning there is no presence to be felt, but the only source of help we should be depending on is God. So, while it is not something people are making a conscious choice to do (except in some religions) people who cling to the memory of a loved one in a spiritual way are walking the fine line of idolatry. And make no mistake about it, this is not pleasing to God. He has commanded that we worship him and him only:

Do not put your trust in princes, in mortal men, who cannot save. ~Psalm 146:3 NLT

Then Jesus said to him, "Be gone, Satan! For it is written, "'You shall worship the Lord your God and him only shall you serve.'" ~Matthew 4:10 ESV

Let everything that has breath praise the Lord! Praise the Lord! ~Psalm 150:6 ESV

Ascribe to the Lord the glory due his name; worship the Lord in the splendor of holiness. ~Psalm 29:2 ESV

You shall have no other gods before me. "You shall not make for yourself a carved image, or any likeness of anything that is in heaven above, or that is in the earth

beneath, or that is in the water under the earth. You shall not bow down to them or serve them, for I the Lord your God am a jealous God, visiting the iniquity of the fathers on the children to the third and the fourth generation of those who hate me, but showing steadfast love to thousands of those who love me and keep my commandments.
~Exodus 20:3-6 ESV

After the death of a loved one, we are weary with grief and vulnerable. The Devil uses these emotions and weaknesses to his advantage. He uses them to try to deceive us and distract us away from God. Don't let this happen to you at any point in time. Just don't.

Part II

The Invisible War

Chapter 12: Satan and His Adversaries

Life goes by at such a rapid pace, don't you agree? And just when we think we've got a handle on things and are in a good rhythm, things abruptly change. It's up to each of us, though, to live and learn with each step. There are always new lessons to learn if we will. Every experience is significant if we let it be, and God uses the good as well as the bad to mold and shape us into the person he created us to be. Sometimes, though, we are close-minded and fail to learn what God wants to teach us. But that's our choice. God has given us the gift of free will and does not make our decisions for us, even though he could if he chose to do so.

Occasionally we will encounter experiences we can't ignore—those that awaken our inner self and challenge our thinking. These are the experiences I consider to be part of God's 'big picture'—something he does in preparation for his greater good (and ours). I consider my experiences at Hazel's to be one of those times, because even though I experienced tremendous fear and anxiety, I grew. I was driven to search for answers and not stop until I found them. That is why I can say with complete honesty, that if it weren't for the fear, I would have blindly continued to believe in God on a superficial level instead of going as deeper and deeper to know him as fully as I possibly can.

I turned to God's words in the Bible to discover where the evil that surrounded me was coming from and why. To some that may seem strange, but to me it made perfect sense since the Bible tells us how evil came to be in the first place, aka *the origin of evil.*

Genesis 1:1 says, "In the beginning, God created the heaven and the earth." God created everything simply by speaking it into existence. That is powerful. It does not say that God created some things, but EVERYTHING…with just a few words.

Over the course of the seven days of creation the Bible mentions multiple times, that everything God created was good! There was no evil during that time. However, in the next chapter Satan appears as we encounter the story of Adam and Eve.

After God created Adam and Eve, he put them in charge of what was to be their home—the Garden of Eden. The garden was full of all kinds of trees bearing good fruit to eat and God gave them permission to eat all of them except for one.

A serpent, who was Satan in disguise, approached

Eve in the garden one day. He tempted her to eat the fruit of the forbidden tree by asking her to question what God said (Genesis 3:1-4). Eve gave into the temptation. She chose to disobey God and eat of the fruit anyway. Her husband did likewise (Genesis 3:5).

Adam and Eve were the first *people* to ever sin. They soon realized, though, that the consequences of their actions were heavy and perpetual. Because of them all future generations inherited their sinful nature (Genesis 3:15, NLT).

Did you notice in the previous paragraph that I specifically said that Adam and Eve were the first people to sin? Not the first of God's creation to sin, but the first people. Satan is the one that introduced sin into God's perfect universe. Satan was originally one of God's angels. His name was Lucifer, which means 'light'. But for whatever reason, he became jealous of the power that God possessed, decided to turn away from God, and actually tried to usurp God's power and authority. As punishment, God banished Lucifer and his cohorts (demons/minions) from heaven and Lucifer from that time forward, was called Satan, which means 'enemy' or 'adversary'.

The Bible goes on to tell us that Satan and the other fallen angels that chose to sin against God are awaiting judgement just as we are. Hell is their end! (Isaiah 14:12-15, NLT, Revelation 12:4, Genesis 6:1-4, Mathew 22:30, NLT, (Jude6, 2Peter 2:4-5, Mathew 25:41). Sadly, it is the end judgement for any and all who choose to be deceived by sin through Satan, instead of delivered from sin by Jesus.

It would have been wonderful if sin would have stopped with Adam and Eve. And to be honest, I have often wondered why it didn't. You would think that their sons and the other people (still not sure how they came to be, but that's for another day) would have learned from Adam and Eve's poor choice. You would have thought they would have warned everyone to not follow in their footsteps. But in the sixth, seventh, and eighth chapters of Genesis, we see that was not the case.

I realize that most of you have heard the story of Noah and the flood a time or two…or two hundred. However, I believe it is worth mentioning again, as it was a key point in my learning process, so here we are.

As time went on and the earth became more populated, sin grew right along with it. The Bible says that things were so bad, God's heart was grieved…broken. He was sorry he had made man at all (see Genesis 6:5-7). To remedy the situation, God decided to destroy all the earth and its inhabitants—except for Noah and his family. God spared Noah because he was righteous and pleasing to God.

God instructed Noah to build the ark, bring the animals, his family, and all the necessary supplies they would need on board, shut the door, sealed it tight, and then proceeded to cause the biggest storm in history. The earth was flooded for a total of 150 days. After the waters receded God made a covenant with Noah—a rainbow in the sky—promising that He would never flood the entire earth ever again.

By God flooding the earth and saving only Noah and his family, did that mean sin had been destroyed? No! There was a time I thought that this would have been true—that God was starting over fresh. But I now understand that when Adam and Eve sinned against God in the Garden of Eden, sin couldn't be undone. Ever. Not on earth, anyway. It would be like trying to put an egg back in its shell after you've cooked it. It can't be done because you can't undo the cooking process. So, because Adam and Eve chose to sin, their pureness was gone from them. Their children and all future generations (including Noah and his family), will have their sinful nature.

I understood that sin wasn't going anywhere, and that God used the practice of sacrifice and the Mosaic Law to accentuate their need for him—to reinforce the truth that on our own, we are completely unable and unworthy of a relationship with God. But one thing about sin surprised me when I started really reading and studying the Bible. I was surprised at how often Satan is mentioned. Not only is he mentioned, but God chose to record more than a few accounts involving Satan's interaction with people, conversations he has with God himself, and his (Satan's) manipulative ways.

I asked myself why would God include Satan and sin in his Word? Why not just stick to the commands and expectations he has for us, and that emphasized his power, glory, and holiness? But then it 'hit' me, which by the way, is 'code' for God giving me the answer to my question. As I began reading, it became more and more evident that we need to know who Satan is, how he operates, and what he is capable of. And more importantly, as I heard a Christian speaker once say, **"…since God's opinion on everything is truth, we need to go to him for every opinion— including who Satan is, how to recognize, him and how to deal with him."**

Exactly! If I was going to depend on God to help me deal with this problem, then I had to know what God's way of dealing with it is…and do it! I also found that the accounts in the Bible involving Satan were things I could easily relate to either in looking at the world in general, or in my own life—the circumstances I was dealing with. I am going to share a few of these with you to emphasize my point. But even more than that, I want you to notice that Satan and his cronies are powerless against God every time!

In Mathew 8:28-34, Jesus came upon two men possessed by demons. He cast them out into a herd of swine. The swine ran down a steep hill and into the sea where they died. The men that kept the swine saw this and went to the city to tell everyone what Jesus had done.

But that's not the whole story. When you read the entire account, you see that the demons actually spoke to Jesus. But what's even more amazing and important is the fact that the demons knew who Jesus was…and were afraid of him!!!!!! Look at what they said:

"What do you want with us, Son of God?" they shouted. "Have you come here to torture us before the appointed time?" ~Mathew 8:29 NIV

The demons knew they were going to lose this battle and that they had already lost the war.

On another occasion Jesus met a crippled woman who had been unable to stand straight up for 18 years. He called her over to him, laid his hands on her, and she was immediately able to stand up straight! She praised God for healing her. (Luke 13:11-13 NLT)

When I think about these people—people whose live experiences God chose to include in the Bible—I am reminded of a time when I visited a friend at the Marquette General Psychiatric Unit. The moment you step out of the elevator, you are greeted with an empty short hallway that curves to the left, and abruptly stops at two steel magnetic doors. To my left there was a red push button intercom blatantly sticking out on a tan blank wall. As I stood staring at those thick steel doors, a creepy feeling swept over me. "Yikes! Do I dare even enter? By the looks of it, nobody is getting in or out unless the person in charge says so," I thought.

My moment of fear was brief as I realized how silly it was to think that way. "I am a visitor, not a patient," I laughed to myself as I boldly, gave the button a push and announced my presence.

Inside, I was met by a nurse who escorted me to my friend's room. Feeling a bit on edge, I glanced around the room, which I assumed to be the lobby. Some patients were sitting quietly watching television. A couple more were walking around repeating sentences to themselves, and a man and woman were arguing with each other about who would get to smoke in the smoking room next.

"Nothing too crazy," I thought to myself, and began to relax. I continued to follow the nurse to my friend's room, which, by the way, was like any other hospital room.

While I was there my friend told me stories of other patients' behaviors he had witnessed so far. Some patients would get so out of hand that the nurses would have to sedate them.

I couldn't help but smile with amusement when my friend said in the most serious tone, "I am afraid that if I spend any more time around these people, I might start acting just like them!"

Thankfully, my friend's stay as a patient was brief and I made it out as a visitor alive, but the experience left a lasting impression on me. The idea that most of the patients would have to be there for an undetermined amount of time (some would never leave), unknowingly existing in a demented state of mind was sad. I can't help but wonder if some of the people deemed 'crazy' are also a victim of an unclean spirit like the ones Jesus healed.

Those thoughts then lead me to wonder if it is

possible that people with less noticeable psychiatric issues like depression, anxiety, and bi-polar disorder are also affected by these spirits in some cases? I know not all, but maybe some?

The Bible tells us that Satan and his demons are among us even now in our earthly world. Think for just a moment what their presence might look like if they weren't invisible to us. Would they be scary? Our society tends to portray evil as frightening, often grotesque creatures. We see evidence of this in movies and books on the subject and have grown accustomed to that label. But do we really know if they look like that? Remember, Satan is a deceiver. He is a mastermind at making sin look innocent and beautiful. Or in Eve's case, tasty.

But no matter how it looks at first glance. Or maybe even a second and third glance, the true ugliness of evil is always revealed because Satan is evil. He can only hide for so long and because evil is, well, *evil*. Its appeal and satisfaction level can't be anything *but* temporary.

Hazel's children and most of the people who worked with me as her caregivers/companions were being deceived. Satan had nearly everyone fooled into thinking that her deceased family members were visiting her before she died so they could assure her that death was nothing to fear. I can see why they wanted to buy into that theory. It was a comforting thought. It made what was happening less scary. But it was not the truth and when we stray from the truth, we are no longer close to God.

I also know why so many people believe in ghosts. They miss their loved one and aren't ready to give them up. But again, what we want can't and won't change the truth according to the Bible.

The Bible clearly states on several occasions and sets of circumstances that death is final for the body and the spirit here on earth—that once we die, we cannot and will not inhibit the earth in any way, shape, or form. But don't just take my word for it. Read it for yourself....

So a man lies down and rises not again; till the heavens are no more he will not awake or be roused out of his sleep.
~Job 14:12 ESV

And just as it is appointed for man to die once, and after that comes judgment. ~Hebrews 9:27 ESV

But now he is dead. Why should I fast? Can I bring him back again? I shall go to him, but he will not return to me.
~2nd Samuel 12:23 ESV

Then man's dust will go back to the earth, returning to what it was, and the spirit will return to the God who gave it. ~Ecclesiastes 12:7 NIV

For the living know that they will die, but the dead know nothing; they have no further reward, and even their name is forgotten. Their love, their hate and their jealousy have long since vanished; never again will they have a part in anything that happens under the sun.
~Ecclesiastes 9:5-6 NIV

No matter what Satan tries to use against us, we have to be on guard 24/7, because most of his advances come to us without notice. He also knows our most vulnerable 'spot' is our emotions. He may seep in slowly a little at a time. He might charge at us full steam ahead, he might wield some high-powered flattery at us, but you can bet that somehow our emotions will be involved. That's because Satan knows the human mind would rather feel than think. It's easier to feel our way through life vs.

thinking our way through. Feeling is easier. It takes less effort on our part, because if we are feeling it, we don't have to entertain the notion that we might be (gasp!) wrong.

The human mind battles daily with what is right and wrong. Satan plants thoughts in our heads, tempting us with things displeasing to God. "Taking this food from my employer's restaurant is ok. He won't even notice it's missing. Besides, he makes good money, is kind of a jerk and does not pay me very much. It's not really stealing.... I work here and um it's not like it is something big. No, he didn't really say it was ok, but it's not a big deal." Or "Go ahead, take a sip of that drink. You have been sober for two years. You can handle it now." Or "Buy the new purse you have been wanting. Who cares if you can't really afford to spend the extra money right now? You deserve it. Isn't that what charge cards are for?" Or "I'm glad Sally lost her job. She was never a very nice person and had it coming to her."

See how easy that is? Satan plants those thoughts, hoping we let them take root. If they do, we let them filter through our hearts into our brains and possibly continue right out our mouth. Even if we don't say them, the fact that we think them and give them our 'seal of approval' is enough.

Satan jumps on that like a mouse that stumbles onto a block of cheese. When the mouse first takes a bite, it is barely noticeable. But the mouse keeps coming back to the cheese, taking bite after bite and before you know it the cheese is gone. Satan is content to get us a bite at a time. He knows that if as long as we don't send him away in the name of Jesus, he's still got a fighting chance. That's why it is absolutely, positively essential that you *know what evil is, recognize it when you see it, call it out, and declare yourself off-limits to it IN THE NAME OF JESUS.*

You don't want to be in the company of evil, do you? If you knew for sure that something was evil, would you associate with it? Be around it? Let it influence you? Likewise, would you respond to good if you know for sure and certain it was good? Would you align yourself with it? Let it be a strong influence on you? Use it to become a better you?

Satan clouds our thinking by making the bad look good and the good look bad (or boring or unpopular). That can't happen, though, if you are deep into Bible study, have a strong prayer life, and surround yourself with Godly people and influences. When you are wise *in* the Lord, you are wise *to* the schemes of Satan.

Chapter 13: God's Army of Heavenly Angels

Angels are a refreshing and positive topic compared to their adversaries! But what comes to mind when you think of angels? Hope? Safety and protection? Beauty, strength, and the grace of God? Those are the most common answers people give. But do we really know if that's correct?

Yes, I think so, according to the accounts of angels we can read in the Bible. Most of us, though, have never seen or encountered an angel—that we know of, anyway. So then, why are they depicted in books, posters, figurines, and even clothes the way they are? You know—the wings, aura of light, and all that? Personally, I am more of the opinion that when God sends his angels to help someone here on earth, they take on a more human likeness, minus the disrespectful parody-bordering-on-sacrilege of what was portrayed in the 1996 movie, "Michael".

"Michael", starring actor John Travolta, is about a couple of tabloid reporters and an 'angel expert' that are sent to investigate the report of an archangel named Michael living with an elderly woman. They find the report to be legit, however the angel is not what they expected. Michael looks like an angel with the big feathers coming out of his back, yet he smokes, drinks, uses bad language, and smells like cookies. (Ephron & Ephron, 1996). I admit I found the movie to be entertaining and quite funny, but as I've already said, it was also very inaccurate. I know that might not seem like a big deal to most people, but it is. It's a big deal because misconceptions lead to misunderstandings, and misunderstandings lead to wrong ideology, aka, believing lies.

Think of it in terms of going to the source for the most accurate facts. You wouldn't consult a third grade PE teacher on how to set up your living trust or will, would you? Nor would you trust your seventeen-year-old son's girlfriend to be the best source of information for the best home healthcare agency to hire to help with your aging parents. So, why on earth would you go anywhere else than the Bible for the most accurate and correct information about angels?

My point, exactly!

The most accurate description of angels can be found in the Bible from which we can draw the following conclusions:

- **Angels were probably created on the sixth day of**

creation: Genesis 2:1
- **God created an innumerable number of angels:** Jeremiah 33:22 and Hebrews 1:14; Hebrews 13:2
- **Angels are subject to God. They work directly for him to carry out his purpose:** 1st Peter 3:22
- **Angels worship God:** Psalm 148:2, 1st Kings 22:19, Revelation 7:11-12, Hebrews 1:6

In Billy Graham's book, *Angels,* he mentions that the Bible refers to angels directly or indirectly almost 300 times! God keeps them busy doing a variety of things. Some were messengers of good news, while others brought warnings. Some were protectors. Some were warriors. Some came to test people's faith. Some came to admonish and discipline. Some came to give comfort, and some were sent to offer companionship.

Here are just a few examples...

The angel of the LORD encamps around those who fear him, and he delivers them. ~Psalm 34:7 KJV

If you make the Most High your dwelling--even the LORD, who is my refuge--then no harm will befall you, no disaster will come near your tent. For he will command his angels concerning you to guard you in all your ways; they will lift you up in their hands, so that you will not strike your foot against a stone. You will tread upon the lion and the cobra; you will trample the great lion and the serpent. ~Psalm 91:9-13 KJV

He protected Daniel from the lions and a fire hot enough to kill those standing several feet away, didn't even leave the smell of smoke on the clothes of Shadrach, Meshach, and Abednego when they were thrown into the middle of it.

An angel brought the news to Abram (Abraham) and Sarai (Sarah) that God was going to allow them to have a child.

An angel visited both Mary and Joseph to tell them of the enormous blessing and responsibility God was laying on them by giving them Jesus to raise. And then later on, angels announced Jesus' birth to the shepherds.

An angel literally had to take Lot and his family by the hand and lead them out of Sodom and Gomorrah.

God also sent an angel to safely remove Peter from prison.

Angels took care of Jesus by bringing him food and water after he had fasted for forty days in the wilderness following his baptism by his cousin John.

Angels told Mary and the other women not to worry—that Jesus was no longer dead. And I have no doubt they will be involved in telling us not to be afraid on the day Jesus returns for the day of judgement.

These are just a few of many examples of the times God's angels interacted with people. From these examples, as well as those that I gave you in which demons interact with people, I want you to be able to accept these three things:

- Angels are real, they acknowledge God's holiness, and they honor, serve, love, and praise him in all they do and say.
- Satan and demons are real, they acknowledge God as being more powerful than they are, and they take every opportunity, and use any and every possible means they can come up with, to weaken and destroy God's presence in the lives of every person on earth.
- Ghosts are not real. Once we die, that's it—until the second coming.

You may be wondering why I took the time to include this information in the telling of my story. But you don't have to wonder, because I'm going to tell you why, right now. Every single day Satan and his demons wage war against God and we are what Satan is fighting to gain control of. He knows he can't beat God. He knows that eventually he will be condemned to the eternal lake of fire. But the stubborn pride that put him in that position in the first place has only gotten stronger and more willful over time, which is why he is going to take as many people with him as possible. He knows that losing will be easier to 'swallow' if he can hurt God in the process by taking as many people with him as possible.

You and I are being fought over. The battle is raging all around, and we need to be able to recognize the enemy, face it head-on, and defeat him with the armor of God protecting us every step of the way. Please take this seriously because it is serious business. Don't ignore or deny the power Satan has to manipulate and deceive you. Don't be like most people, (56% according to research done by the Barna group a few years ago), who think Satan is just a symbol—not a real being.

I'm not trying to scare you or freak you out. But I do want you to be scared of what can happen if you aren't alert and on guard. Satan has only one goal: To keep us away from God and he is relentless in his pursuit.

I know some of these things seem harmless or 'just the way things are', but that's exactly what Satan wants us to think. He wants us to think that the movies, video games, music lyrics, and magazines aren't bad. He wants us to continue to ignore the vulgar language, nudity, sex, and violence that just keeps getting worse in these venues, and society in general. These things are all just accepted without giving them a second thought.

Satan's existence is also evident in the number of crimes committed, addictive and abusive behaviors, the breakdown of the family, and the overall attitude of selfishness, anger, and discord among people. Yet over time we have become desensitized to it all—just the way Satan wants us to.

But God sure hasn't! It doesn't please God to see unhappiness and dysfunction in our lives. He wants better for us. He has better for us. All we have to do is ask him and then stay close enough to him to receive and enjoy it.

That being said, although Satan has a hand in our lives, he cannot be blamed for everything bad that happens. Satan cannot cause us to do anything bad. He doesn't have that much power. All he can do is throw temptation after temptation at us. But what we do with them is completely up to us. That means for good or bad, our circumstances are of our own making, which I believe happens in one of two ways. Way number one: We are human and make mistakes.

For example, have you ever locked your keys in the car? Spilled coffee on your nice shirt? It wouldn't be realistic to blame such things on Satan. These things are nothing more than unfortunate accidents or negative consequences of making poor choices. Like choosing to try to balance your coffee on the slopped roof of your car while you buckle your toddler into their seat...while the wind is blowing. Way number two: Times when God finds it necessary to discipline us for being disobedient to Him. A good example of this is found in Haggai 1:6-9. God challenged the people to consider their ways...

"You look for much, but behold, it comes to little; when you bring it home, I blow it away. Why?" declares the Lord of hosts, "Because of My house which lies desolate..." NIV

So, how do we know when Satan is attacking us? There is no one single answer to that question. Satan is very tricky. He is referred to in the Bible as a deceiver and "the Father of lies (John 8:44)." We are also told that sometimes Satan will pretend to be good and even pretend to be one of God's angels...

For such men are false apostles, deceitful workmen, masquerading as apostles of Christ. And no wonder, for Satan himself masquerades as an angel of light.
~2nd Corinthians 11:13-14 NIV

When I saw the two ladies in Hazel's garage, I believe Satan was trying to trick me. The cheerful blond lady was wearing a white short-sleeve shirt with white capris and it made me think that she could have been an angel. The other lady, whose back was to me, was wearing all dark clothing. I wondered if she was of the Devil. Neither of the ladies was real, as in human, but the difference in their clothing made me wonder if they were battling spirits.

God tells us to test the evil spirits to find out if they are of him or of the devil, so that verse alone tells us that both are real, *and* that we will be approached and exposed to both. God doesn't just tell us to test the spirits and leave us hanging. Through Paul, he tells us how to test them.

If a spirit acknowledges that Jesus Christ was sent to earth as a human by God, then the spirit is from God. If the spirit does not acknowledge this happening, or disowns Christ as Savior, then the spirit, according to 1st John 4:1-3, is of the antichrist.

Satan doesn't always use a direct approach in disowning Christ as Savior. Sometimes Satan is a fence straddle or line walker. He sticks close to what is true and good in order to make you think that what he is saying or doing is true. He even tried this trick on Jesus. After Jesus had fasted for forty days, the book of Matthew (chapter 4) tells us that Satan came to Jesus; tempting him when he was physically weaker than most of us will ever be. He tempted him by twisting the words of the Psalmist. He was mostly right. He only left out a few words, but the words he left out completely changed the meaning of the Psalmist's words. Jesus didn't fall for it though because he knew the Word. He wasn't unaware of Satan's capabilities or his tenacity. We, too, can (and should) be shielded by the shield of faith and know how to effectively use the sword of the Spirit (the Bible) as described in Ephesians 6:10-18.

Satan also uses the tactic of planting doubt in your heart and mind. When Eve was in the Garden of Eden, the serpent was trying to get her to question what God said by saying, "Did God really say, 'You must not eat from any tree in the garden'?" (Genesis 3:1). And as we all know, Eve fell for it hook, line, and sinker. Despite the fact that she and Adam were in direct communication with God. They were in a relationship with God like no one else ever has been. Yet from what we read, there is no indication that she hesitated for even a moment!

On one hand that seems impossible. How could she *not* hesitate? How could she be so gullible? But aren't we? Don't we fall hook, line, and sinker for Satan's tricks more times than we care to admit? Despite the fact that we have the Bible, which is full of warnings, advice, and encouragement not to? Despite the fact that we have preachers and teachers, and people like me who are willing to share their life experiences in hopes others will learn from them?

Yes, we have all of those things, yet it still happens. It can happen in a heartbeat when we let our guard down. I know because it has happened to me. Once, while reading my Bible, thoughts came into my head along the lines of, "Who does God think he is that we should worship him?" "Why does he think he is better than anyone else?" These thoughts frightened me. I knew they were not my own. I know without a doubt Satan had dangled them there to tempt me away from God by doubting God.

Another thing you need to know is that Satan is equally sneaky about the timing of his temptations. He waits and watches for the perfect time to try to put temptations in our way for us to trip and fall over; taking a faceplant into sin. Chip Ingram, in his book, *The Invisible War*, writes that there are five specific times we can expect a spiritual attack from Satan. They are:

1. Spiritual Growth (when we are getting closer to God).
2. Invading Enemy Territory (such as sharing our faith with others)
3. Exposing the Enemy (revealing truths about Satan)
4. Breaking with the World (such as repenting sin)
5. Blessings to Come (times that God is using you for his glory)
(118-121)

When I took a few minutes to stop and think about this list, I realized Mr. Ingram is right. Each of these times greatly increases the probability of an attack from Satan. He knows that the closer we get to God, his chances of adding one more to his 'team' gets smaller. I also knew it was accurate because I was living it.

When I discovered the truth about the ghosts at Hazels being demons, I began to grow spiritually. That growth—my deeper relationship with God is also why I decided to write this book. It was not written for the sake of sensationalizing my experiences or to create a shock-effect. Its primary purpose is exposing Satan for who and what he is. Evil. Wicked. Antichrist. Eternal separator from God.

But before I go into more detail on that, I want to tell you about the night things changed—the night I claimed victory in Jesus over Satan and his demons.

I want to start by saying that God gave ALL believers the power to cast out demons in His name (Mark 16:17, Luke 10:19). I know that sounds outlandish. Maybe even ridiculous. But it's not. You also need to remember that God wouldn't have bothered talking about it or giving us that ability if the possibility didn't exist that we would need it. He knows what Satan is capable of and of his relentless personality.

No matter whether the demonic influence is a temptation you are teetering on or an all-out attack on your soul like I (and countless others) have experienced, you and I…we *all* have the ability to cast them out of our lives. All we need is faith!

Jesus told his disciples that they only need faith equal to the size of a grain of mustard seed (Mathew 17:20) to get the job done. That sure didn't sound like much, and quite honestly, I felt like my faith was bigger than a seed, so after learning about this Biblical truth from the Pastor and his wife, I decided to give spending the night at Hazel's another try.

I can't truthfully say my faith was big enough to be

absolutely, positively certain I could cast out the demons in Jesus' name, but I knew I had to try. I knew in my heart of hearts that the faith that said God would protect me no matter what—would be enough. And it was. My faith *was* enough. *I experienced victory in Jesus that nigh*t!

I saw for myself that even though Satan is strong, God is stronger! My experience that first night back at Hazel's was tangible proof that Satan is no match for God and that he flees at the very mention of Jesus's name.

I'm not going to tell you it was easy-peasy-lemon-squeezy. The fear that started brewing inside of me my first night back at Hazels was *almost* overwhelming. I was fine at first, but as the evening wore on, I started getting nervous. By bedtime, I was a nervous wreck. And sure enough, the demons came. I knew they would. There was no way Satan was going to pass up the opportunity to try to stomp my faith into the ground.

By the power and grace of God, though, that's not the way things went down. I took a deep breath, asked God for courage and strength, and then I *demanded* in the name of Jesus that the demons leave. I *demanded* that they leave me alone and leave the house.

In the time it took me to take another deep breath, they were gone. I could literally feel the weight of the evil lifting off of me and being replaced by a sense of calm and peace. I, myself, cannot think of any words to adequately describe how magnificent and awestruck I felt. But when I think about that night, the words to a song by Chris Tomlin come to mind. Here are the words to the chorus of the song. They come closer to explaining how I felt…how I still feel that anything else I could say.

Indescribable, uncontainable…
…All powerful, untamable,
Awestruck we fall to our knees as we humbly proclaim
You are amazing God….

Had it not been for God's mighty and holy intervention, I would never have been able to sleep after such an ordeal, but I did. I didn't just sleep. I slept peacefully. Just like David did in Psalm 4:8, when he said, *"In peace I will lie down and sleep, for you alone, LORD, make me dwell in safety." (NIV)* After that night I continued to spend nights at Hazel's, and my faith increased as I learned that God is always there for me. Always!

Chapter 14: Relentless Pursuit... Relentless Protection

Don't think that after that night it was over—that Satan gave up and moved on to someone else. He doesn't work like that. He is relentless in his pursuit. God, however, is also relentless in providing protection against his adversary.

After that night at Hazel's I knew that I was empowered by the Spirit to be protected against and to stand up to Satan and his demons. I knew I could demand in the name of Jesus for them to leave and they would. For a while, anyway. Until they thought I might have left my guard down a bit, or that I might be in a frame of mind to give up or get tired of God not doing what I felt was enough.

Sorry, not sorry to disappoint you, Satan, but that's not how I felt. Each time I experienced victory over Satan and his demons, my faith grew stronger. Was I frightened? Yes, at times. Was I concerned about what they might try next when they realized they were no longer being successful? Yes, I was. But I didn't let those things get the best of me. I *chose* faith over fear.

The demons came in the night, but I stood firm

against them; demanding they leave in the name of Jesus. Each and every time they did; proving more and more that they are limited in their power.

Knowing these limitations exist is empowering to me, and should be to you, too. Knowing God is mightier and more powerful than Satan should cause us to run to him and join ourselves to him. To do anything else or less just doesn't make sense. Think about it—who purposely chooses to be defeated? No one, that's who!!

I also feel obligated to tell you that when I started writing this book, the attacks against me intensified. One example of how this happened took place one day as I was typing some notes for the book on my laptop. I took a break to do something, and when I came back, I looked at the screen and saw a page and a half of continual six's staring back at me! Revelation 13:18 tells us that the number 666 is the devil's number:

This calls for wisdom. If anyone has insight, let him calculate the number of the beast, for it is man's number.
His number is 666.

What's more, before I started writing, the attacks only occurred at Hazel's house. Once I started writing, though, my husband and I also both began experiencing Satan's attacks in *our* home. It became normal to be awakened in the middle of the night to the blanket being pulled off our bed, getting tapped on the head, and hearing the demons walk around our house talking.

It was terrifying to realize that the demons weren't contained to Hazel's house. I don't really know why I thought they were. Or maybe the better way to say that, is to say I assumed they were bothering me because I was at Hazel's. I naively assumed they wouldn't leave Hazel's house—that I was nothing more than a plaything for them because I was there. It never occurred to me until the first night they attacked me at home, that *I* was the target—that *I* was the battle trophy. They weren't attacking me because I was at Hazel's. They were at Hazel's because they were after me!!!!!!!!

The first night my husband heard and felt the presence of the demons was a night I will never forget. He was scared, mad, confused, and at a complete loss to know what to say or do. I don't think I have to tell you why he was scared and what he was sacred of. His confusion and uncertainty in knowing what to say and do, don't really need any explanation, either. The first time or two you experience something like this it is terrifying. It is also a bit surreal. You know it's real, but you don't want to believe it's real. Why? Because if you believe it's real, then it is.

And *that* means all your perceptions about Satan and hell being something church people say to scare you, are null and void.

I have to tell you, though, that when my husband experienced these things with me, I was more than a little bit relieved. I know that sounds odd, but if you will remember what I said earlier, he was extremely skeptical of the whole thing. He thought I was imagining things or blowing whatever was happening way out of proportion. But once he experienced and saw these things happening for himself, he knew I wasn't imagining anything. He knew it was as real as real can get, and he was terrified.

One particularly unsettling incident took place one night when I got up to feed our third child when he was a baby. After feeding him and putting him back to bed, I laid down on the couch. Right after I laid down, I heard a "click." It sounded as if someone had just turned our stove on in the kitchen. You know what I'm talking about, don't you? It's a gas stove with burners you ignite and then turn back to the amount of flame you want.

Anyway, because I'm a mom, I couldn't convince myself that it was nothing. So I got up to look. Sure enough, the oven was on! Our stove was old and whenever the oven was on, the left back burner would heat up as well.

A kitchen towel was lying two inches away from that burner! I moved the towel, turned the knob off and went back to lie down on the couch. I was barely settled when I heard it again. "Click!" I ran into the kitchen to find it on again. "They are trying to kill us!" I thought.

The next morning, I called my dad on the phone to ask him if there was any possible way that our stove could have malfunctioned and turned itself on. He said that it was not possible, because as we both knew, you have to push the knob in and then turn it in order for the burners to light. I knew before I even called Dad what his answer would be. I just needed a little more convincing that I wasn't being paranoid.

Another time I was attacked by Satan in such a disturbing way that I am actually a bit reluctant to share it with you. I have started typing out the details of the incident more than a few times over the course of writing this book but have deleted them each time. I've prayed about it and then asked myself if telling you will be giving Satan the attention he is after, or if it will give you another sizeable piece of evidence proving just how real and evil he is. Finally I decided to quit praying for God to let me figure it out and start praying that God would clearly tell me what he wanted me to do; specifically whether or not he wanted me to include the incident in the book. It wasn't an instantaneous response, but before too long I had a sense of peace and assurance from the Holy Spirit telling me to include the incident in the book.

The truth that sugar coating or ignoring what happened will actually be a disservice to you. It would also be giving Satan what he wants, which is to seem harmless and benign. So, (this is me taking a really deep breath and letting it out reallllllllllly slow) I am going to share with you the most frightening experience of my life.

I had been up late working on this book. Too tired to type, another word, I settled down in my bed at about 1:00 a.m. I don't think my head had even hit the pillow when I had a vision of myself standing in the bathroom in front of the sink. I glanced down to see blood coming out of my wrists as if I had cut them. I looked up and saw blood gushing out of my mouth. And then it was gone. As quick as the vision started, it was over. Or at least the image in my mind was, but emotionally and spiritually, it was anything *but* over.

I felt an oppressive weight of heaviness and hopelessness in the room. It was literally so heavy that I struggled to lift myself up off the bed, but I had to. I knew I had to get Satan and his demons out of our home! I had never in my life been troubled with depression of any kind. No teenage anxiety. No issues with body image or self-esteem. No post-partum depression. Nothing like that. Fear? You betcha! Who isn't afraid from time to time? And as the pages of this book have told you, I had plenty of things to scare me. Had I felt uncertainty and anxiousness about encountering demons? Again, you betcha! But depression or doubts about wanting to live? No way! Not even remotely. Not ever.

Remember back to what I told you when I babysat for the little boy all those years ago? I was willing to deal with it on my own rather than risk being labeled a crazy teenager. Yes, I repressed a lot of memories of demonic incidents for several years, but they in no way held me back from excelling academically, or from having healthy relationships and being a great mom to my kids. This was NOT me going crazy or falling into a state of depression! This was an all-out attack by Satan for my soul! And he was NOT going to win!!!!!

When I finally lifted myself up off the bed, I went around the house and cast the demons out; demanding in the name of Jesus that they leave us alone! I told Satan he was NOT going to stop me—that God was my source of strength. My defense. My protector. I declared in the name of Jesus that Satan would not win this one and that I was no longer fearful of him or his demons. They could do nothing to me that God could not and would not save me from.

I just sighed another huge sigh of relief. It feels good to finally tell you these things—both the bad and the good. Now I just hope and pray you understand and appreciate the gravity of what happened. By sharing this experience with you I hope you understand the length Satan will go in his efforts to take someone away from God.

But not this time. Not me or my family!

I knew after that night that Satan was going to do his best to keep me from writing this book. He doesn't want me to expose him for what he truly is. The bad press will be bad for business, you might say. But if Satan was that upset, then I couldn't help but feel the Spirit's blessing to keep going, because if only one person is saved because of it (although I hope and pray it will be many, many more), then it will be worth everything I've been through.

Satan didn't earn the title of adversary by rolling over and giving up easily. He cannot overpower God and God never gives up on us or gives in to Satan. But that doesn't stop Satan from throwing punch after punch to try to get *us* to give up—which is what he did with me.

After that night of declaring that my family and I

were suited up in the armor of God and that God was leading the charge, things still continued to happen. Things that frightened me. Things that caused me to wonder if I was going to be able to fight the fight. Things that threatened my marriage. Things that caused me to wonder incessantly why me. For example…

On more than one occasion as I was typing the pages of this book on my computer, I would notice that somehow all the Bible verses I included were messed up. The words would be out of place. The rest of my story, however, would be intact. One time I spent almost two hours trying to fix them, but every time I would get partway through, they would suddenly be jumbled again. I was very frustrated and wanted to think it was some sort of computer glitch, but I knew differently.

Another time I was talking on the phone with my friend Rietta (the one from the outhouse story at the beginning of the book). Rietta knew what had been taking place, how I had come to rely heavily on my faith and relationship with Jesus to deal with it all. That was actually why we were having the conversation. She said a co-worker of hers, who was not a Christian, was struggling with what she believed to be demonic influences. She said she'd called because she wanted to talk to this co-worker about Jesus and wanted some input from me about what to tell her.

I was glad to help. So I started telling her about some of the most recent events and how I demanded in the name of Jesus that the demons leave…and that they did. As I was talking to her, she mentioned the music that was playing. I didn't hear any music, but she insisted that strange music was playing in the background.

Rietta was also interested in my story and my goal of writing a book to help others. I asked if she would be willing to take a look at what I'd written so far and give me some feedback—constructive criticism, you might say. I wanted to know if she thought it was something people would actually want to read and something that might actually help someone. She said she'd be happy to, so I printed off a hard copy of what I'd done to that point and mailed it to her.

Not long after the manuscript arrived at Rietta's house, odd things started to happen that creeped Rietta and her husband out. A few of her knick-knacks flew off a shelf, and other things moved from one place to another. Her husband said, "Maybe you better send Christa's book back to her!"

And then there were those times like…

Early one winter morning, I got up with my husband to say goodbye as he left for work. As I sleepily watched my husband walk out the door to his snow-covered car, I shut the door behind him and locked it. As soon as I did, I heard a man's voice behind me yell, "Hey!" It sent chills up my spine. I don't believe my husband had even left the driveway yet so there was still time to run out and stop him. I decided that there would be nothing he could do because I knew the man was not human. Instead, I decided to cast the demon out in Jesus's name. Later, I was telling my husband what had happened when he left that morning on the phone and he heard strange music playing on the phone (like Rietta did). I didn't hear anything but his voice.

As you can imagine, the stress level in our home was…high.

Whenever we would be awakened by the demons talking, walking, pulling blankets off the bed, tapping us, or breathing on us, my husband was as afraid as I was. He would tell me to cast the demons out and I would. At first we would spend the rest of the night awake just waiting for them to come back—with extra lights on in the house, of course. But as my faith grew and I realized that Jesus really had sent them packing, I would climb back in bed and fall back asleep almost immediately.

This infuriated my husband. "How can you go back to sleep after all that?" he would wake me up angrily. I would tell him that Jesus took care of them. "Yes, but what if they come back?" he says. "Well if they come back, then we will cast them out again," I would say and turn over to go back to sleep.

He couldn't wrap his head around that at the time and would stay up for hours waiting for the next thing to happen. He still hasn't come to terms with things—not really. The reason for this is because he no longer has a relationship with Jesus. I am NOT saying that judgmentally. I'm just stating facts. We had attended church together when we were dating and after we got married, but at this point in time my husband was angry with God.

He was angry because he had not been able to save his dad, who was and is his forever best friend. He and his dad hunted together, went fishing together…they did everything together. But on April 28th of 2003, my father in-law had a heart attack and died. My husband tried to revive him but couldn't.

Since then he has been angry with God. He no longer attends church, and as far as I know, he has no relationship with God. I have tried to tell him that I am just as afraid as he is when the demons attack, but that Jesus takes the fear and replaces it with peace and assurance—the peace and assurance that lets me go back to sleep. It doesn't matter, though. He says I need to just keep doing "my thing". He has seen my faith grow, and he has witnessed the demons leaving when I demand they leave in Jesus' name, but he still doesn't want a personal relationship with Jesus.

I also know he blames me for the demonic presence in our house. I can't argue that point. Nothing happened in our home until I decided to write this book. I often stayed up late working on it. It was easier to concentrate then. The kids were in bed, the house was quiet, and the words just seemed to flow more easily. As I was working on the book, demons would attack my husband while sleeping alone in our bed. It doesn't take much of an imagination to figure out this was not a good thing. He was incredibly angry with me and did not want me to write my book at all.

His attitude and feelings put me between a rock and a hard place. I didn't want to put any more stress on our marriage than there already was (demons have a tendency to stress a marriage), but since they were working so hard to keep me from writing the book, I knew they saw it as a huge threat. When I sat down and explained how important this was to me and why, he said that while he wasn't happy about it, he understood and agreed it was the right thing for me to do.

It was also at this point in time that the demons switched up their tactics. For the most part, they left me alone (except for messing with my book manuscript). Most of their attacks were on my husband. Even more upsetting was that they usually waited until he was alone in the house, or at home with the kids while I was gone. It didn't take much for me to figure out why they did this. If I weren't home, they couldn't be cast out because he wouldn't do it.

This was the case while I was out shopping late during the Christmas Black Friday sales a few years ago. He called me around 10:30 that night and said I needed to come home because the kids were sleeping, and the demons were walking around our house. So, I came home. When I got there, I saw that he had every light on in the house. To this day he will not stay home alone at night. One time the kids and I went away for the weekend and he slept in his car in the Walmart parking lot. I told him the demons could come to the Walmart parking lot as easily as they could to our house, but if he would stand up to them in the name of

Jesus, they would leave.

    Was I not proof of that? Were things not better for me? Yes, and yes, but he was not convinced.

Chapter 15: God is Always There

One day I made a quick stop at the grocery store to pick up a couple things. As I headed for the checkout, I noticed an elderly man resting on a chair near the bakery.

"So that's what was making all those little noises I heard throughout the store," he smiled. He was pointing at the car seat in my cart containing my 10-month-old boy.

"Yes, he likes to talk a lot," I said.

"I have two kids of my own and my wife and I have been raising our 14-year-old granddaughter since she was a baby," he said, then continued telling me about his life. It was obvious he was desperate to get some things off his chest.

In a few short minutes I learned that his son and his granddaughter's mother were drug addicts; making them unfit to raise their little girl. Additionally, because of the mother's drug use during pregnancy, the granddaughter had been born with an array of health problems.

"It's just not fair!" he continued. "The girl's eyes are so bad; she can barely see anything in front of her. I asked the doctors if they could give her my eyes, but they said they couldn't. I would do anything for that girl!" he said solemnly.

He obviously loved his granddaughter, but the years had been difficult. His zest for life and energy were waning quickly. He had become a shell of a man whose tired eyes matched the story he told.

I was just about to tell him I would be praying for them, and invite them to church, when he said something I was not prepared to hear. The elderly man lowered his head and whispered, "I am going to put an end to my life soon. It is just a matter of when and how. The only thing holding me back is that it will devastate my granddaughter."

I had been in a hurry to get in and out of the store, but in that moment, time stood still. This man was pouring his heart out to me…a stranger! I knew this wasn't an accident or coincidence. God put me there to help that man. I know he did because if he really wanted to end his life, he wouldn't have told me he was going to. He was crying out for help and God used me to intervene.

I wasn't sure what to say or do, so I said the first thing that came to mind, "You are your granddaughter's world. She and your wife would be devastated. Please don't do that!"

I wish I could tell you I know for sure and for certain what happened, but I don't. I hope and pray with all my heart he chose life and that somehow my simple reminder that he was loved and needed was enough. I guess I'll never know for sure, but here is something I *do* know. I know no one's life is an accident. We were all planned at the same time God said the first, "Let there be…." Each of us is uniquely designed in the womb. God creates each and every one of us with a specific purpose in mind. You and I are alive because it is God's will (Revelation 4:11).

To be alive is a gift from God! Sure, life can be difficult and bad things, even horrendous things happen. When these things happen, our first inclination is to wonder why God allows such things. I know I have, and I probably will do it again in the future. But when those thoughts start to creep in, I ask God to bring me back to his way of thinking. To help me get there I think about a comment I read once that said, "Don't ask 'why me'. Ask 'what can I learn from this."

If we take the time to stop and think about it, we really don't have to ask why bad things happen. We should realize these things happen because one) we live in a fallen, imperfect world, and two) we sin. In other words, some of what we go through is because sin is in the world, while some things are the result of our own personal sin. Addiction and abortion are sins of our choosing. Covid-19 and confrontations by demons are because of sin in general.

God uses both, however, to test our faith, reveal his holy and almighty character to us, and to help us grow and mature in our relationship with him.

I recently met a man whose story is a perfect example of both kinds of 'why' when it comes to bad things that happen. I'm not exactly sure what his real name is. I just know he goes by Eagle Man, so I will call him Eagle Man, too.

Eagleman lost his daddy when he was only three years old; leaving him and his siblings to be raised in poverty by a mom whose only concern was where her next drink or hit was coming from.

As a child, Eagleman would drink whatever was left in the glasses his mom and her friends left lying around when they passed out. By the time he was in junior high, he was, in his words, "addicted to 'more'. More drugs. More alcohol. More things to steal to buy more drugs and alcohol...."

He also had trouble coming to terms with the fact that his mom decided she wanted more out of life, too. But not more alcohol and drugs. She wanted more *than* those things. So, she cleaned up her act, went to school, and got a degree that led to her career as a licensed substance abuse counselor.

As a counselor she was unable to help her son, though, until he wanted to help himself.

Fortunately, Eagleman came to that point. He had what he calls an epiphany one night while he was at a party. At the ripe old age of sixteen, the young addict looked around the room at all the filth, depravity, and hopelessness and realized he may as well be looking in a mirror. He was one of…of *them!*

This realization was enough for him to set his drink on the table and walk out the door. He walked out with the intention of never going back there again; 'there' being high, drunk, and engaged in criminal activity.

Unfortunately, it wasn't that easy for him. Eagleman relapsed ten times in thirty-six years. He spent time in hospital beds, rehab facilities, and jails.

Eagleman wanted to get clean and stay that way, but it wasn't until he realized he couldn't do it on his own— that he got serious about the popular twelve-step program for addiction recovery. The program teaches that God must be involved in the process of healing and recovery. This was an alien thought process to Eagleman because he did not believe in God. His thoughts were more along the line of "If there was such a God, he is obviously not concerned with my life in any way whatsoever."

It took eight years for him to realize God is real and that he loves Eagleman as dearly as he loves anyone.

Today, Eagleman has an amazing relationship with God. He says, "When I was using, I thought I was entitled to a better life. I was wrong. I thank God daily for my wife, hot water, a warm house, food, and gas in my truck. I thank him for everything every single day."

Eagleman is also allowing God to use him to help others with their recovery from addiction. He meets with people to talk, drives them to meetings/treatment centers, and helps make coffee and clean up after meetings.

If you ask him about his relapses over the years, Eagleman says he can now view those times as preparations for him to help others—to give them hope when they relapse and have to start over…again.

"If I never touched a hot stove," he says, "I would not be able to tell others not to touch a hot stove because I wouldn't know why they shouldn't."

I love Eagleman's story because it is such a vivid example of both reasons for why bad things happen. Eagleman was a victim of his surroundings as a child. The sin he was surrounded by and entrenched in were not his fault or of his making. But…when he decided to participate in those sins and make them his lifestyle of choice, he wasn't just surrounded by sin. He was choosing sin.

Even more beautiful is how we see the power of God's love at work in the world. Even when we choose sin, as long as there is breath in our body, we can un-choose sin and choose God. He never says no. He never tells us we've messed up too many times.

Yes, there are serious damning consequences for those who *deliberately* keep on sinning, and yes, he wants us to remain repentant and obedient. But he also knows the difference between being deliberately disobedient and dependency. He knows and he lovingly protects and heals us from our sin when we let him.

The other thing you need to know about sin is this: **no matter what the sin is or why it becomes part of your life, Satan is at the root of it.** Satan is the initiator of all sin. He thrives on it, and he wants you to die because of it. The Bible tells us that we can expect to experience many attacks from Satan throughout our life. Mathew 12: 43-45 warns us not to let our guard down because of his constant attempts to take us down.

And don't think it can't happen to you. Nobody is immune to the vices of Satan. Even Jesus, who was perfect, experienced attacks from Satan! The only time we can be certain that Satan will no longer bother us is when we die or Jesus returns! Until this happens, the invisible (and not so invisible) war will continue to be waged and we are all right smack dab in the middle of it.

That's it. That's my story and I'm stickin' to it—my purpose for sharing my story with you. It's not about trying to scare you or trying to sound like I have some mystical connection with the underworld. It's not about making you paranoid or trying to convince you that you are being watched and taunted by invisible beings. My purpose for telling my story is to let you know that a war *is being waged* by Satan and:

- He wants nothing more than to make you an eternal casualty
- His weapons of warfare can be both subtle and astoundingly dramatic
- His weapons of warfare are always meant to inflict pain, suffering, and spiritual death

Satan repeatedly strikes each of us when and where we are most vulnerable. Why Satan chose to wage war with me the way he did, I will probably never know. He may or may not choose to do the same with you. But like I said—that's not the point. The point is to make you aware of the **reality and voracity of Satan**—no matter what weapons he uses.

The other message I want you to get from all of this

is to **believe in God and *know* God—the God who won't desert you. The God who made it possible for you to have victory because of Jesus.**

Part III

Victory In Jesus

Chapter 16: Jesus, the Victor

The battle is real, but so is the reality of who has already won the war. That's right—countless battles are being fought every single minute of every single day. Why? Because Satan is a sore loser. He knows he is the loser, but he is determined to take as many of us down with him as possible. This is sad…tragic. But the winner has already been declared. Who is it?

Drum roll please! The winner is…… God! Satan and sin were defeated when God sent Jesus to die on the cross:

For God so loved the world that he gave his one and only Son, that whoever believes in him shall not perish but have eternal life. ~John 3:16 KJV

Jesus loves us so much that he *chose* to be obedient—to endure horrible persecution and death to save us from Satan's destruction and from the eternal punishment of hell. It wasn't his death that saved us. Or rather, not *only* his death. It was Jesus' victory over death—his coming back to life—that sealed the deal. And when we choose to follow him in faithful obedience by accepting the gift of salvation and the blessed responsibilities and privileges that go with it, we will live with him eternally in Heaven. (Acts 2:38; John 14:6; Acts 4:12; Romans 1:16; Romans 6:23; 2nd Corinthians 5:21; 1st John 5:13; Mark 16:15-16)

I know it's hard to comprehend at times—especially when we look at everything happening around us. We can't deny that the world is getting progressively worse—almost on a daily basis. It is also hard, given the condition of society, not to think that Satan is winning. But make no mistake about it—Satan is only here because God allows him to be. Or as Billy Graham wrote in his book "Angels", *"Satan is indeed capable of doing supernatural things-but he acts only by the permissive will of God; he is on a leash"* (14).

God promises us time and again that one day Satan's wickedness will be revealed, and he will overthrow him 'with the breath of his mouth' (2nd Thessalonians 2:7-9).

I am glad of that promise, along with all the other promises God made. I am glad because God is the ultimate promise keeper. His words are truer than true. I also look forward to the day when we no longer have to worry about Satan and his plots and schemes because of God's promise to return. Only God knows when that will be, but that's okay with me. He said it will happen and that's enough for me. I'm not one of those people who tries to figure it out. I choose to use my time making sure I'm always living in 'ready-mode'. I'm not concerned about when it happens. Instead, I focus on living each day in 'ready mode'.

For me, being in 'ready mode' has come to mean that when I get up each morning I put on the full **Armor of God.** The armor of God is the arsenal of weapons God gives to anyone and everyone who chooses to be his child. Have you ever been to a park where a bunch of people were wearing t-shirts that said something like, "Widener Reunion" or "One of the nuts on the Lewis family tree"? Well, the armor of God is, you might say, our family reunion t-shirt. Only better. Much better. And something we can wear every day without having to toss it in the laundry.

If you aren't familiar with the armor of God, take a few minutes and read this a couple of times to let it sink in. If you *are* familiar with it, take the time to make sure your armor is securely in place so that you are as prepared and protected as you can possibly be.

Finally, be strong in the Lord and in his mighty power. Put on the full armor of God so that you can take your stand against the devil's schemes. For our struggle is not against flesh and blood, but against the rulers, against the authorities, against the powers of this dark world and against the spiritual forces of evil in the heavenly realms. Therefore put on the full armor of God, so that when the day of evil comes, you may be able to stand your ground, and after you have done everything, to stand. Stand firm then, with the belt of truth buckled around your waist, with the breastplate of righteousness in place, and with your feet fitted with the readiness that comes from the gospel of peace. In addition to all this, take up the shield of faith, with which you can extinguish all the flaming arrows of the evil one. Take the helmet of salvation and the sword of the Spirit, which is the word of God. ~Ephesians 6:10-17

    Do you see what God was doing when he told Paul what to write? God uses the example of a soldier preparing for battle to teach and to warn us to be ready to fight against sin and evil. But God doesn't just tell us what weapons to use, he tells us how to use them. And even before that, he makes sure we know who and what we are fighting against and who and what we are fighting for.

    From these verses we learn that we are fighting Satan and his force of demons. His weapons are temptation, deceit, lies, pride, greed, and all those things that look so innocent and appealing…until they aren't.

God understands that the most effective way the battles Satan wages against us is to have a fail-proof battle plan. A plan that a) knows who the enemy is b) acknowledges the enemy's strengths c) finds the enemy's weakness d) includes being ready for anything—including the unexpected and e) is executed by a fully-trained and fully-equipped soldier.

The concept of being fully equipped cannot be missed here. God covers the entire body with his armor. The feet, which move us in whatever direction we choose to go. The heart, which rules our emotions and filters our thoughts. Our head, which is where our wisdom, logic, and reasoning comes from. Our body/vital organs, which are what keep us functioning.

When I first read about the Armor of God in Ephesians, the mental image that came to mind was that of a knight from Medieval times. I pictured a knight dressed head to toe in heavy metal plates strong enough to resist any spear or arrow that may be fired against him. I imagined a shield in one hand and a metal helmet atop his head with small thin slits for the eyes. Such an outfit would be heavy, cumbersome, and downright awkward. And can you just imagine what it would have been like in the summer?!

Thankfully, we don't have to put all those things on to fight with Satan. But the comparisons God makes are good reminders. No, they are vital reminders of how to 'dress' from the inside out in order to fight and win against Satan's constant assaults.

Just like countries prepared for war, we need to be prepared in our fight against Satan, lest we be defeated by him. When I think about battling Satan, I am relieved, thankful, and comforted to know I am not alone—that I have the Holy Spirit in me leading the way. Sometimes, though, I am overwhelmed with awe over the fact that God cares enough about each of us as individuals to do that. Especially when I think about how often I've disappointed him and rejected him to do things my way. But then he reminds me that his willingness to love me so fiercely and in spite of the mistakes I make is not all that different than my love for my own children. It's like he whispers in my ear, "You would do anything to protect your children, wouldn't you? So would I."

I once heard a story that puts it into perspective. It was a fable about a baby who was taken by a dragon and placed in a tall tower at the top of a tall mountain. The mother begged and pleaded for anyone in the village to rescue her baby. So, the strong men from the village traversed the mountain but failed to rescue the baby. And the army of the village ventured toward the mountain but failed as well. Everyone told her "It cannot be done; your baby cannot be rescued."

One day the mother decided she could not stand one more day of being separated from her child, so she braved the mountain and climbed the tower. When she returned to the village that night, she was carrying her baby in her arms. Everyone stared in awe and disbelief. The strong men and the armies of the village failed in their efforts. "How did YOU, a weak frail woman climb that tall mountain and scale that tall tower and rescue the baby?" they asked.

The mother replied, "It wasn't THEIR baby." (Kami Dempsey, 2015)

As a mom, I can totally relate to this story. I would do anything to keep my kids safe. I've lost countless hours of sleep caring for and watching over them. I kiss their boo boos. I sacrifice my time and interests in order to put their needs first. I will do whatever I can to show them love and protect them. I would die for them!

But even though my love for them is unconditional, it is not perfect. I make mistakes almost every day. I lose my patience, favor one child over another, and get upset with them too easily when something else is on my mind. Sometimes I am just too tired to deal with everything the way I should. There are also times when I am overprotective or fail to discipline them when they need it. I have also been known to bribe my two year with a sucker in exchange for peace and quiet in a grocery store. I could go on, but you get the point.

God's love, on the other hand, is both unconditional and perfect. That doesn't mean there is never discipline, reprimands, or a firm, "No, because I said so." That's as it should be, though, because perfect love isn't just all warm and fuzzy. It's firm, fair, and fuzzy. We don't deserve God's love. We don't deserve the hope of heaven. We can't earn it or aspire to it. It is a gift from God through Jesus to us.

When we accept Jesus Christ as our Savior, we are made new/born again. Our outward appearance remains the same, but God gives us his Spirit, the Holy Spirit, to live in us. The job of the Holy Spirit is to guide, protect, reveal, and teach those in whom he lives. That doesn't mean we won't ever struggle or sin because we will. Just like any child disobeys from time to time, we disobey our Father, God, from time to time. But as a Christian, we should have the desire to develop a close and intimate relationship with him through prayer, Bible study, learning from those who are more mature in Christ, through service, praise, worship, and fellowship with our brothers and sisters in Christ. Accepting Jesus as Lord and Savior is not difficult, but it is life changing. It is a promise to give back to God what he gave you…*your life.* According to the Bible accepting Jesus as your Lord and Savior happens when you…

At one time we too were foolish, disobedient, deceived and enslaved by all kinds of passions and pleasures. We lived in malice and envy, being hated and hating one another. But when the kindness and love of God our Savior appeared, he saved us, not because of righteous things we had done, but because of his mercy. He saved us through the washing of rebirth and renewal by the Holy Spirit. ~Titus 3:3-5 NIV

Therefore let all Israel be assured of this: God has made this Jesus, whom you crucified, both Lord and Messiah." When the people heard this, they were cut to the heart and said to Peter and the other apostles, "Brothers, what shall we do?" Peter replied, "Repent and be baptized, every one of you, in the name of Jesus Christ for the forgiveness of

your sins. And you will receive the gift of the Holy Spirit.
~Acts 2:36-38 NIV

Jesus answered him, "Truly, truly, I say to you, unless one is born again he cannot see the kingdom of God."
~John 3:3 ESV

Because, if you confess with your mouth that Jesus is Lord and believe in your heart that God raised him from the dead, you will be saved. ~Romans 10:9 ESV

Then he brought them out and said, "Sirs, what must I do to be saved?" And they said, "Believe in the Lord Jesus, and you will be saved, you and your household." And they spoke the word of the Lord to him and to all who were in his house. And he took them the same hour of the night and washed their wounds; and he was baptized at once, he and all his family. ~Acts 16:30-33 ESV

As I had previously mentioned, prior to the encounters with Satan's demons, I had never read the entire Bible. I knew reading the Bible was important and it was something I planned to get around to 'someday.' But honestly, I wasn't sold on the claims that it was the greatest book ever written. I am not proud to say I found parts of it quite boring compared to several other books I read. My experiences at Hazels, however, were the 'wakeup call' I needed. I needed answers. I was desperate for answers. Thankfully, I had enough church background to know the Bible was where I would find the answers I was looking for. So that is where I went, and I was not disappointed.

    I don't want to imply it was easy or instantaneous because it wasn't. At first I had trouble understanding some of what I read. I didn't give up, though. I knew there was too much at stake. But then the same can be said for everyone. Our very souls and eternal destiny are at stake, so don't give up. As long as you actively seek God, you will find him because he is always ready and waiting to be found.

    As I continued to read, the Bible came alive. I spent hours jumping from one book to another, writing verses down as I went along. It was as if I was reading the Bible for the first time and I couldn't get enough of it. Today I can proudly say, "The Bible is the greatest book ever written!"

Prayer also satisfies our hunger and quenches our thirst. Prayer, aka talking to God, enables us to develop a more intimate relationship with him. Think about it—do you know of any healthy relationship that exists without communication? Me, either. Communication is a must if we want to get to know God better. Even though God knows all things, he needs us to talk to him. Conversing with God is proof that we recognize God as God—the one who is the supplier of every need and blessing.

Prayer has always been a weakness for me because I found it difficult to talk to someone I could not see. I worried that my prayers weren't beautiful and poetic like the ones I have heard other people pray. As my relationship with God developed though, I realized the prayers God wants are those that come from our heart. Remember—God knows our every thought and desire, so why would we pray anything different?

Jesus tells us in his Sermon on the Mount (Matthew chapters 5-7) that we should pray for direction in our lives, thank God for all he is and does, ask him for forgiveness, pray for the needs of others to be met, and for our own needs and desires. Sometimes it may seem as if our prayers go unanswered, but you need to know that the only prayers that go unanswered are the prayers we do not pray. If you pray it, though, God answers. Sometimes he says no, sometimes he says yes, and sometimes he says wait because it's not time yet. But rest assured, God does answer every prayer you pray.

Chapter 18: Are you Lost

Most of us can recall a time in our life where we had been lost at some point or another. One of my most vivid memories of being lost was when my sister and I decided to take the Greyhound bus from Rapid River, Michigan to Nevada, Missouri to visit our mom. I was twenty-two and my sister was fourteen. I was looking forward to just riding. No following a map. No stopping to pump gas. Just riding. Unfortunately, the trip didn't go as smoothly as I anticipated.

By car, we would have reached my mom's house in about sixteen hours. By bus it took almost twice that long. We had been given a schedule of stops, bus changes, and layover times when we bought our tickets. Three words: What a joke! The bus drivers didn't know what a schedule was. One of our buses ended up being an hour and a half late because he stopped along the way to visit with friends. They had to re-route our entire trip and we had no idea where we were going or what bus we had to be on and when. It was a total nightmare! An unpleasant experience…to say the least.

A lot of people (possibly even you) are living their entire lives in that same state of 'lost'. Even more astounding is that a lot of the time they don't even know it. Or care. Living in the moment or thinking you are either invincible or that 'someday' is too far off to think about is the general mindset. In some small measure that is okay. We aren't supposed to *worry* about tomorrow. We are supposed to trust God to guide us through each day. But we are also supposed to be good stewards of what God gives us and of our lives. We are supposed to live life *here* in preparation for eternity.

    I know from experience how hard this can be. I still don't have it down pat. I mess up on a regular basis; getting off-track by the distractions in life. You know—things like kids, family, work, money…. But I know what I need to do, and I am now (thank God) at a place in my life that I recognize when this happens, so I can stop, drop to my knees (literally or figuratively), and pray for help to get back to where I need to be.

    I know how easy it is to feel that there are not enough hours in a day to accomplish everything that needs to be done. I know it doesn't take much for priorities to get out of whack. That's why it is essential we start each day knowing where our priorities SHOULD be: God first, yourself (you have to love yourself before you can love others), your spouse, your kids, and your extended family (including your church family). I know this is true. I also know how easy it is to let it get off-balanced. And if you are like me, the first thing to suffer is almost always my relationship with God—the very thing that is supposed to be number one, because it is the thing that keeps everything else right and good.

It's not intentional. It happens gradually without my noticing it. But again—that subtly is one of Satan's 'best' tricks. For example, my kids might get sick; resulting in me getting less sleep and having less energy. I forget to pray once and then I do it less and less. Before I know it, I find myself not praying at all. Or maybe I get busy with my business or running to the kid's baseball games. I'm tired, so I let my Bible reading go one day to answer emails. Then the next, and the next…. You get the picture! Becoming distracted is easy and Satan delights in our distractions. **Living for God is a conscious choice we must make every single day.** It can be a battle, but it's one worth fighting. Trust me!

Earlier in the book I mentioned that I officially accepted Jesus as Lord and Savior when I was nine years old. I spent most of my life after that knowing about God and trying to do the right thing, but I never really took the time to get to *know him personally*. I guess you could say that God's existence in my life was abstract. I pictured him far away, watching me up from Heaven, judging my every move. I also knew that simply being good (obeying the law, being kind, etc.) isn't what gets you to heaven—that it is a relationship with God and being obedient and faithful that was the 'key'. Yet it was not a priority for me. I had my own goals and dreams. I planned on living my life for myself and making the best of it. In other words, I knew, but I didn't care. Like so many other people, the here and now…a life that I could plan for and envision was what mattered most. And then along came Hazel.

My experiences at Hazel's house turned my world upside down. Dealing with the demons was like a nightmare I couldn't wake up from. But then I did wake up—spiritually speaking. With the help of a few mature Christians who prayed for me, walked me through God's Word, counseled me, and encouraged me, I was able to turn the nightmare into victory. My terrifying interactions with Satan led me straight into the arms of God. The God who had been there the whole time, but whom I had ignored until…until I didn't. Instead of scaring me *away from* God, Satan scared me straight *to* God.

I'm far from perfect. My life is far from perfect. My faith is far from perfect. But I am continually being molded, shaped, and led by The Perfect and Holy One True God. What was God's abstract existence in my life is now God's concrete presence in my life. I have put my faith in him, fully knowing that my life is a gift, and my purpose in life is to live for him. I still have my own dreams and goals, but my greatest desire is that God uses my life to fulfill his purpose in the world.

    I still face the same struggles that everyone else does. But now when bad things happen, wonder, "What is God up to?" I have complete faith in him. I know that he is working behind the scenes and that his plan is flawless. Everything in life will happen according to his perfect will and for my good.

    Are you lost? Are you wandering around trying to find what you once had? What you see in someone else? If so, the 'place' you need to go is God. God will work all things for his glory and your good if you let him. But you have to choose. You can choose God, or you can choose to deny him. No one else can make or live the choice for you. My prayer is that by reading this book you have come to believe and comprehend the reality of both good and evil and the fact that we are either on one side of things or the other. I also pray with a sincere heart that you choose good. That you choose God.

Chapter 19: Tell Others

I know I've already said it a couple of times, but as I sit here typing this final chapter, I want to say once more, that my purpose in opening myself and my family's life up to you has been done with the sincerest of motives—to point you to Jesus. It hasn't been easy to do. This account of how Satan came after me full force in ways not often heard or talked about, has opened me and my family up to a great deal of scrutiny and skepticism. One example of this is my 'friends'.

After I took the all-important step of claiming the power of Jesus to get rid of the demons, I wanted to talk about it—to tell people how real the power of God really is. Not with just anyone. I wasn't ready for that. No way! But surely I could tell my friends, right? Surely they would be supportive of me. Curious, confused, and possibly even scared, too, but supportive…right? Not so much.

I was part of a Mom's of Preschoolers group who got together at each other's homes to let the kids play while we visited, ate junk food, and did some fun activities. I had gotten especially close to four of the other moms, so I decided to tell them what had happened and how I had found the faith and courage to deal with it. Afterwards, three of the moms ghosted me big time. The fourth one soon followed. Everyone was suddenly too busy to get together.

I finally got up the courage to ask one of them why I was suddenly the outcast. She said, "We don't really have anything in common with you anymore. You're…different." When I asked another mom, she said they just all preferred to stay home now.

I knew she wasn't telling the truth. I knew it was because of what I shared with the four women I thought were my friends. Talk about feeling alienated! They looked at me like I was crazy. They wouldn't even have anything to do with me when we saw each other out and about in town. The rejection was painful. I hurt for me, but I also hurt for my kids. I couldn't tell them we weren't playing with their friends anymore because Mommy was being stalked by demons, so they just had to wonder why.

But I know whom I have believed in and that he (God) is able to keep me and my family from all harm. He already has and will continue to do so as I faithfully obey his desire for me to use my life to bring glory and honor to his Holy Name.

I won't lie. I've thought about quitting and sharing this with only those I know I can trust. It's not easy to deal with the nastiness Satan still throws at us knowing my husband's faith is not strong. I have also struggled with the possibility of the attention that will be cast my direction once the book is published. Will people think I'm just trying to get attention? That I'm looking for my day in the spotlight? And how will I respond? My daily prayer concerning these matters is to pray the words of Jesus in Matthew 5:14-16 which says…

You are the light of the world. A town built on a hill cannot be hidden. Neither do people light a lamp and put it under a bowl. Instead they put it on its stand, and it gives light to everyone in the house. In the same way, let your light shine before others, that they may see your good deeds and glorify your Father in heaven. NIV

Sharing this story with you is my way to be a light of the world so that you and I can both glorify God the Father in heaven for his power, protection, and victory over sin and Satan.

Final Thoughts

I am happy to say that I no longer live in fear of Satan and his demonic forces. That's not to say I am not fearful of Satan himself, because I am. I know first-hand that he will stop at nothing to destroy your confidence, your sense of well-being, and your mental, emotional, and spiritual stability. I also can't say this is over. As long as Satan feels he doesn't have you where he wants you, he keeps at it.

Satan uses a number of different tactics to get to us. He uses fear and intimidation. He uses the allure of money, popularity/fame, prestige, sex, unhealthy relationships, temporary satisfaction from substances, and material possessions. He plays on our grief, pride, weaknesses, and our lack of knowledge and understanding of God's ways. He uses all of these things; depending on what he thinks will be most effective. And if you give him an inch, he'll take a mile. Or as the Bible calls it in Ephesians 4:27, a foothold.

Some of the ways Satan continues to taunt and intimidate me include demons entering the homes of my two brothers. Strange voices, shadowy figures, and a cut gas line on their cook stove are a few things they have done. Prior to these events, I had talked to both of them about what was going on, so I cannot help but think these things are due to Satan's pursuit of me. He continues to put roadblocks up where this book is concerned. There have been otherwise unexplainable incidents involving people trying to harm me. People have tried to tear our family apart. He continues to send demons to try to frighten me from time to time.

BUT...

Satan cannot succeed if you don't let him, though. He cannot do any more than he is allowed to. But we are no match for him on our own. God needs to be the one to lead the charge against him. God must lead because he has the stamina to stay the course. And God is faithful to do just that.

Throughout all of this, my deepest fear, greatest concern, and most earnest prayer has been (and continues to be) that God will keep a protective hedge around our children. God has honored that; something for which I am eternally grateful. Only our oldest, who is in his early teens, knows what this book is about and why I am writing it. It hasn't been easy for him to come to terms with it—mostly due to his fear of what might happen—but as I said, God is faithful and is honoring my heart's desire to not allow

Satan to touch my kids. Not now. Not like this. Not because of me.

Going forward my goal is to share my story with as many people as possible. To as many as will listen. NOT for a shock-effect or to promote intrigue in the supernatural or the dark world of demonic activity. The Bible clearly speaks against such things. My purpose for speaking up and speaking out is to warn you to be on guard against anything that pulls you away from God and his truth, because anything, and I mean anything, that pulls you away from God on any level and to any extent is the work of Satan. So please…please draw near to God so he will draw (and stay) near to you.

References

Barna Group. *Barna Examines Trends in 14 Religious Factors over 20 years*
> https://www.barna.com/research/most-american-christians-do-not-believe-that-satan-or-the-holy-spirit-exist/

Dempsey, Kami. (2015). Baby locked in a tower by dragons. (Speech). It Works! Conference
> Limelite 2015. Tampa, Florida.

Dexter, P., & Quinlan, J. (Writers). (1996). *Michael* (Motion picture). United States: New Line
> Cinema. Ephron, N. (Director), Ephron, N., & Ephron, D. (Producers)

Eckhardt, John. *Prayers that Rout Demons & Break Curses*. 2nd ed. Lake Mary, FL. Charisma. 2010. 62, 97-98. Print.

Graham, Billy. *Angels: God's Secret Agents*. 3rd ed. Dallas, Tx. Word, 1994. 23. Print
---. *The Holy Spirit*. 2nd ed. Nashville. Word. 1988. 165-174. Print.

Ingram, Chip. *The Invisible War: What Every Believer Need to Know about Satan, Demons, and Spiritual Warfare*. Grand Rapids: Baker, 2006. 61. Print.

Story, Laura. (2002). Indescribable. Recorded by Chris Tomlin. Copyright 2015 Sixsteprecords/Sparrow Records.

"What God tells us in the Bible about trying to communicate with the dead, ghosts, with other spirits, reincarnation, psychics and aliens." *The Young Earth Creation Club.* 21 October 2010.